For: Dr. Heath

William T. Jones

11-20-06

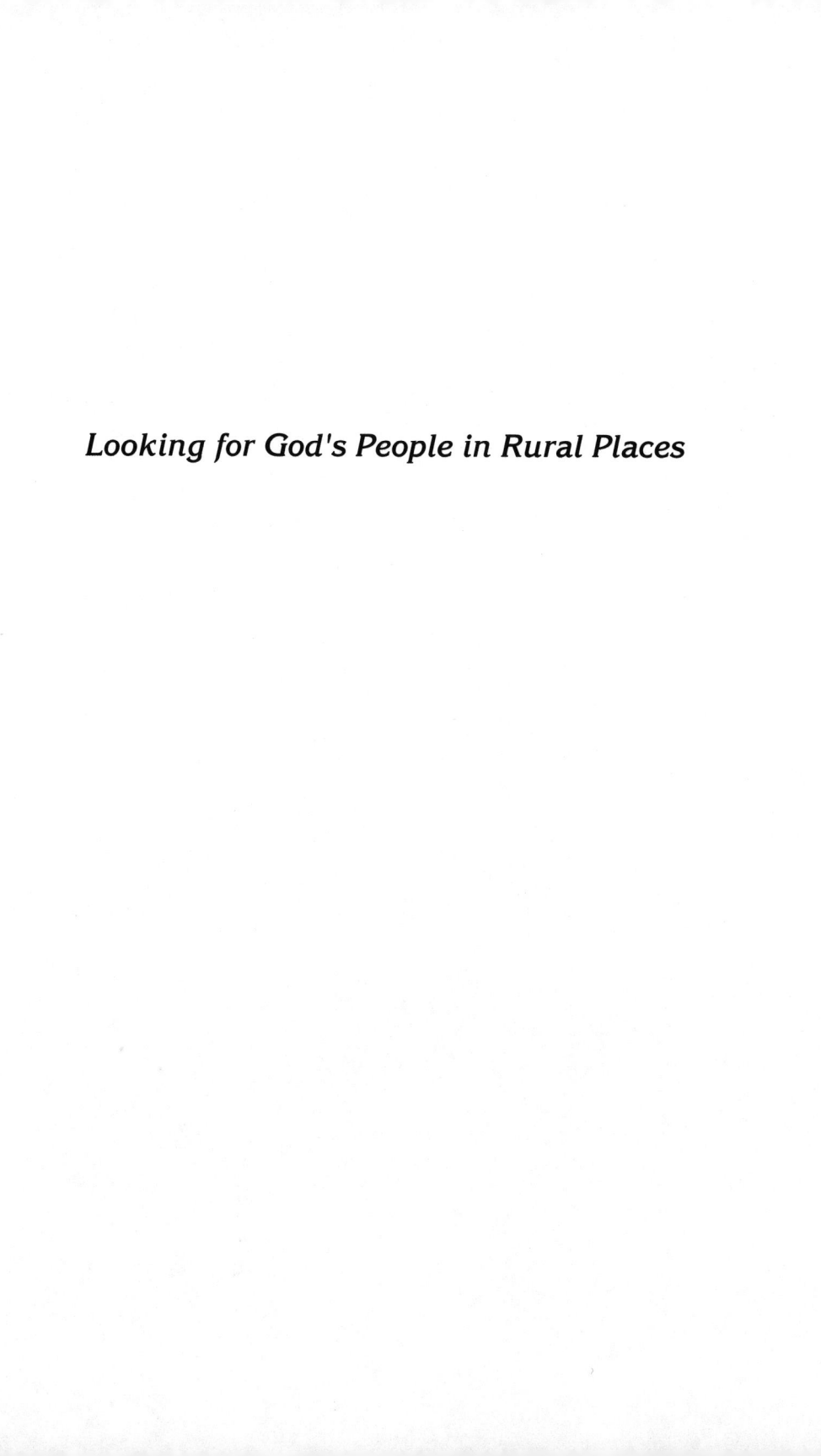

Looking for God's People in Rural Places

Looking for God's People in Rural Places

William H. Jones, D.Min.

Foreword by
Robert L. Satcher, Sr., Ph.D.

Brunswick Publishing
Lawrenceville, Virginia

Copyright © 2005 by William H. Jones
All rights reserved under International and Pan-American Copyright Conventions. No part of this book my be reproduced in any form or by any means, electronic or mechanical, including photocopying or by any informational storage or retrieval systems, without written permission from the author and the publisher, except by a reviewer who may quote brief passages in a review.

Library of Congress Cataloging-in-Publication Data

Jones, William H. 1938-
 Looking for God's people in rural places /
William H. Jones ; foreword by Robert L. Satcher, Sr.
  p. cm.
 Includes bibliographical references.
 ISBN 1-55618-206-6 (hardcover : alk. paper)
  1. Rural churches. I. Title.

BV638.J66 2004
2 3'.09173'4--dc25
                              2004057033

First Edition
Published in the United States of America
by

Brunswick Publishing Corporation
1386 Lawrenceville Plank Road
Lawrenceville, Virginia 23868

In memory of

**Bishop Lincoln Augustus Baker Berry
September 22, 1927 – January 17, 2003**

My pastor and brother in Christ who taught me that spiritual sensitivity is a gift from God, and whose brief life and death were a part of my preparation for God's call to rural ministry. He meant more to me than he knew.

Table of Contents

FOREWORD BY ROBERT L. SATCHER, SR., PH.D.	9
ACKNOWLEDGMENTS	11
PREFACE	17
CHAPTER 1 Ministering in the Highways and Hedges	1
CHAPTER 2 The Impact of the Rural Church	16
CHAPTER 3 The Search for New Life	24
CHAPTER 4 Life in the Rural Church and Community	33
CHAPTER 5 The Importance of Pastoral Counseling	43
CHAPTER 6 The Mission of the Rural Church Within the Community	51
CHAPTER 7 The Significance of Faith	56
CHAPTER 8 Preaching in the Rural Church: Two Sermons	61
Feeding the Lambs and Sheep	65
A Decision Must Be Made	73

THE CONCLUSION	80
ENDNOTES	82
SELECTED BIBLIOGRAPHY	95

Foreword

A "bolt of lighting" in spirituality, is what can be said of Doctor Jones' book, *Looking for God's People in Rural Places*. He has "hit a home run," so to speak in delivering, perhaps, a first serious look at an area of the Church that can help all churches come to grips in our soul searching, for an understanding of the vital and creative role of the rural church.

One of the most important facts about churches is that they are not all alike; though, all churches continually aspire and search for effective ways of carrying-out God's will on earth. Doctor Jones brings on a new perspective from the quiet solitude and spacious surrounding which is typically the backdrop of the rural church.

Some unusually good background information is presented; which is undergirded with biblical and historical facts and research. Then, the author unfolds with some great sermons. He speaks with authority on the rural church. We can all learn from his backlog of experiences, and the interpretations of his experiences.

He lets us know though Christianity is the highest profession in the world, with an open invitation to all without regards to status or background; that there is no distinction in the sight of God; that God's people in the rural churches have a clear and unequivocal challenge. Perhaps the pace is slower, giving rise to much forethought and timely contemplation.

There is yet much to be said about "God's People In Rural Places"; however, the author has a unique vantage from the standpoint of his background and experience of living and the rural setting, and serving in the rural church. His devotion and commitment to the overall viability and serviceability of the rural church uniquely qualifies him to write about it.

His book, *Looking for God's People in Rural Places,* comes at a time of urgent need, when many churches are "groping in the dark" for definition and identity. Indeed, the rural church has an unquestionable identity and a rather clear vision of its role. I am confident that faithful and dedicated Christians everywhere will benefit and find comfort as they read and digest, *Looking for God's People in Rural Places.*

ROBERT L. SATCHER, SR., PH.D.
Professor of Chemistry
St. Paul's College
Lawrenceville, VA 23868

Acknowledgments

Trust in the Lord with all your heart, and do not rely on your own insight. In all your ways acknowledge Him, and He will make straight your paths.
— Proverbs 3:5-6

There seems to be no end to writing books. But there are few books with distinct, relevant, and directive messages. Such books are difficult to write. They demand an imaginative and creative mind. They blaze new trails for the daring pioneers to explore in this business. This book is a result of a concern for the rural church and community that has been growing in me for a number of years. The process for writing it has been for me a spiritual experience. It is hoped, however, that in some small way the publication of this book will be helpful to readers from a wide range of Christian traditions, and I hope they will find this work both stimulating and inspiring. I do not think I have taken up many "extreme" or "sectarian" positions, but I have tried to bring to expression the broad mainstream of rural America's thought for *Looking for God's People in Rural Places*.

Until recently, little has been written about the rural church in America. Most publications address the growing, large, or super church. This book is an effort to contribute to a better understanding of communicating the Gospel of Jesus Christ in America's rural church and community. However, this book is not presented as if the intended reader does not know anything about the subject. My hope is that many of the reader's own beliefs will be confirmed, some unarticulated thought clarified, and perhaps some new ideas discovered or stimulated in the process.

It is my desire that this book will provide ministers and lay Christians with insights designed to bring about change also, to help the rural church and community adjust to the way the Gospel of Jesus Christ is communicated to them. The rationales outlined in this book can be utilized by any church ministry desiring to look for God's people regardless of its size or location.

My deepest appreciation is warmly given to those who have made this book possible. I thank God for opening up the windows of heaven and pouring out blessings on me. There are many people who have influenced my Christian life over the years. To those of you I have left out, please forgive me.

No book is written without collaboration. I am indebted to those who have written books and articles that have provided me with new thoughts and stimulated me to work even harder at shaping thoughts of my own that are still not formed.

The footnotes and references are primarily intended to make such acknowledgments but may also serve the special interests of those who wish to explore a particular interest in more detail. Unless otherwise indicated, Scripture quotations are from the Revised Standard Version of the Bible, copyrighted 1956 and 1952.

When I began to develop my dissertation for the Doctor of Ministry degree at Howard University School of Divinity, I had no questions about what the topic would be. I entitled it, "Communicating The Gospel Of Jesus Christ In America's Rural Church And Community." What follows in this book is a spin-off of that dissertation. The first three chapters of this book are revised editions of the first three chapters of the dissertation. The other chapters are new creations that emerged from my research and *Looking for God's People in Rural Places.*

A word of gratitude is due and gladly acknowledged to Dr. Lawrence N. Jones, Dean-Emeritus of Howard University School of Divinity. I am grateful to Mrs. Barbara W. Coles, Mr. John W. Lewis, and Mrs. Trudy J. Lewis who proofread this manuscript. It is a pleasure to also acknowledge the dedicated commitment to editorial typing by Mrs. Lunette T. Ellis. Their observations and suggestions have been very valuable to me. I am indebted to the Rural Ministry Institute of Washington, D.C., for their professional courtesy that contributed significantly to this book.

The persons who have influenced my Christian life over the years are the late Sister Otelia Moss Lewis, my grandmother, and Dr. Monroe R. Saunders, Sr., Chief Apostle of the United Churches of Jesus Christ (Apostolic) and my former pastor and mentor, the late Bishop Lincoln A. Berry. Their wisdom and teaching have had a tremendous impact on my life. I thank God for these ANGELS. I express my personal appreciation to Great Branch United Church of Jesus Christ (Apostolic) family for their openness, support, and prayers as I labored for ways to look for God's people in rural places. As a new and growing church, their response to my ministry in both words and deeds have been a continual source of inspiration and motivation to prepare this manuscript for publication.

Most books of this nature are usually dedicated to people with whom we have a "primal" that is familial relationship: to mother and father; to wife, husband, or beloved; to daughters, and sons; and or sisters and brothers. Relationships of this nature create, shape, and uphold us as persons; they also constitute the greatest base of joy and fulfillment in life. For that reason, I will not deviate from that practice.

No one has been more supportive to my work than my family, Rochann and Trudy (my daughters), Randy (my son) and John (my son-in-law). Without their love, encouragement, and prayers, I would never have completed this work.

I owe most of all, from a human perspective, to my wife, Queen Ester, whose prayers, loyalty, and confidence from the beginning that I would complete this manuscript and get it published sustained me. She has listened and loved me through it all. Thank you for not turning your back on me when I doubted myself and being a friend in every sense of the word. It is to my wife, Queen Ester, that this book is dedicated.

Finally, I must acknowledge my profound thanks to my Lord and Savior Jesus Christ, the Almighty, to whose glory this effort is offered, and through whose merciful providence, this book was brought to completion.

NOTE: Throughout this book I have tried to limit the number of gender-designating pronouns and other forms of sexist language. However, when the context indicated the need for a singular noun or pronoun, I chose to use a masculine term, rather than "his or her," or other more cumbersome conventions. I trust that this choice results in a more readable text. I also trust that this choice is not offensive to the reader; no offense or irresponsible disregard for current editorial style is intended.

Preface

> *Do your best to present yourself to God as one approved, a workman who has no need to be ashamed, rightly handling the word of truth.*
> – 2 Timothy 2:15

The writing of books requires many gifts, all of them coming from God, but most of them are experienced through other people. At two turning points in my life, the teachings of my pastor and friend Dr. Monroe R. Saunders, Sr., The Chief Apostle of the United Church of Jesus Christ (Apostolic), and personal support of my wife, Queen Ester Maclin Jones, helped me to gain perspective on what it means to be a servant called by God to teach and to preach His Word. The greatest gifts have been those of acceptance and understanding from those who best know me as a person, my children, Rochann, Trudy, and Randy.

The purpose of this book is to present in a self-conscious way my understanding of rural ministry on an in-depth level. In the process of writing this book, I reflectively dealt with the subject of *Looking For God's People In Rural Places*. This work includes the following concerns:

I. The Rural Minister as Person and the Community of Faith

    A. Pastor as Prophet: How can the roles be integrated theologically and procedurally?

    B. Pietist and Activist: How can the two be reconciled in the rural church?

    C. Alienation and Community: What is the minister called to understand and do in the face of those who radically differ with their ministry?

    D. Administration as Ministry: What is the theological ethical foundation of good administration, and how does administration relate to the work of the pastor and prophet?

II. The Community of Faith and the Wider Community

    A. Religion in a Secular Age: What does the rural church have to say?

    B. The Shared Ministry: Who are the servants of God in the modern world? What is the unique mission of the rural church?

    C. The Generalized and the Specialized: Conflict or complement?

    D. Sectarianism and the Churches: What is the meaning of growth for one and the declining appeal for the other?

E. New Forms of the Church: What are the forces in the rural church today that call for them, and what qualities must the rural church leadership possess?

F. New Fields of Mission: What are some of the missionary frontiers of our time?

   a) The rural ethos about small church ministry.

   b) The urbanized countryside.

   c) Crises of function and authority in government.

   d) The development debate at home: lifestyles and life quality.

   e) The crisis of meaning in rural America: affluence and poverty.

III. Theology in the Service of Contemporaries

   A. In rural America, issues in this category revolve around basic choices among theological stances related to apparent human needs on the one hand and apparent fidelity to Christian heritage on the other. However, these are all in a practical framework included in the rural minister's responsibility for developing his own style of ministry while serving in the rural church and community.

The rural minister's faith is an integral part of his life and profession. Faith in that which constantly reminds him that he is a son of God that is always assisting the quality of self-acceptance that both push and allow him to continue to stay fully in touch with every aspect of his spirituality. The minister's faith will find its expression in personal relationships in ways that are appropriate for each situation he encounters and faith that facilitates openness in the sharing of his ministry in the rural church and community.

The Bible makes it very clear in (John 15:16) that Jesus said to his disciples, "You did not choose me, I have chosen you and appointed you that you should go and bear fruit and that your fruit should abide; so that whatever you ask the Father in my name, he may give it to you." To be a rural minister is to be unlike anyone in any other profession or calling.

A rural minister wears many hats. For example, "he is an evangelist. He is a religious administrator. He is a social reformer. He is a director of worthwhile enterprises for the community. He is a species of an amateur psychiatrist. He is an educator. He is an interpreter of life somewhat in the fashion of the poet. The rural minister is a custodian of the values of a democratic civilization."[1] The rural minister is also a person of superior wisdom and virtue whose tasks are daily to demonstrate to men, women, boys, and girls how to live more wisely and virtuously. With all these titles or jobs, one can understand why young rural ministers and some of the not so young ministers find themselves dragged in a dozen different directions as they try to fulfill the calling of their ministries. As an administrator, the rural minister must, in the fullest sense, speak a language that God's people will understand; in other words, feed them fresh bread at each meal, and yet at the same time be the minister of Jesus Christ with a ministry based firmly on what he has learned of the ministry of Jesus Christ in the first century.

People in the rural community tend to have more confidence in the minister who gives notice to meetings, who sends informative letters, and who issues reports, especially the financial ones. If the minister does not inform the membership, someone else may misinform them. His sermon time must be for preaching almost 100 percent of the time. However, there will be times when he must let the Bible speak for him and be the authority on specific crises within the Church and within the community.

With authority, the rural minister must demonstrate the Scripture by his lifestyle. The Bible will not come alive in the Church membership's daily lives unless they allow it to be a part of their thinking, their actions, and their conversations.

Ministers in rural areas must keep the Church in touch with the interchurch movements. Cooperative relationships and programs will enrich the Church. The rural minister, as administrator, who limits association with other organizations, will curtail the overall effectiveness of the Church. In spite of this, members are often critical of their "much traveled" minister, who must keep on the move to help the rural church stay in touch with the "world" he is called out to "save."

Cooperating ministers stabilize congregations and help them find shelter in the time of crisis, stress, and storms within the Church and community. This kind of relationship and fellowship can fulfill this promise, "For we are his workmanship, created in Christ Jesus for good works, which God prepared beforehand, that we should walk in them" (Ephesians 2:10).

One of the most effective ways for the rural church minister to lead God's people is through the decentralizing of power. Power in the rural church must be shared. The rural minister must be an enabler or an equipper, one who helps stimulate dreams and provide leadership. He must be able to create power centers to make dreams a reality. He must be trained and experienced in his profession so that the congregation may become as creative as possible, making them totally responsible for their actions. This whole process of being creative and responsible is undergirded with positive affirmation and assurance that allow one to make mistakes and still be creative in the process.

Many questions came to my mind as I endeavored to find effective ways to look for God's people in rural places. Questions such as, what are the characteristics of the rural church? What does rural mean? Does it refer merely to geography? Are there social, political, educational, and economic issues that are peculiar to "rural people?" Does counseling differ in the rural context as opposed to other contexts? Are there distinctive ways that a rural church can utilize the particular talents, experiences, and skills of its members in addressing problems characterizing the geographic area in which they reside? How can the Gospel be utilized in meeting the needs of rural people, both within the Church and within the community? Will the Gospel help rural people grow in understanding, both in the personal and social dimensions of Jesus Christ as their Lord and Savior? What are some of the ways in which the rural minister must communicate to persuade rural people to make a personal commitment to Jesus? How can the Bible and other religious materials be used in communicating the Gospel to the rural church and community? What skills are needed to effectively communicate and demonstrate the love of God to his people? What are some of the daily crises confronting the rural community? How can the minister insure the survival of the rural church? Will the rural community gain better insights in communicating the Gospel by looking at religions of the world? Are there issues in education and schools that impact rural people in distinctive ways? Has the rural church any interest in these matters as a community dedicated to God's will and purpose? These unanswered questions have inspired me to examine the relationship between communicating the Gospel, culture, and theories and defending communication as the transmission of information, ideals, emotions, and skills by the use of symbols, words, pictures, figures, and graphics. Other theories explain communication as being the vehicle by which power is exerted. Simply stated, communication is to make clear God's message to His people.

Rural ministry efforts vary with the geography, social setting, culture, and climate of the rural regions within America. The conditions of the ministry vary from place to place. There has been a tendency to identify rural with one or more characteristics such as agriculture, small scale, backward, or country. It is quite possible to attach a positive meaning to the word rural. Protagonist of the rural church and community interests often identify rural with honest, straightforward, hard working, friendly, outspoken, and independent.

The rural church considers the community to be the geographical area in which the Church is located and the place where the Church directs its evangelical outreach. However, a community may be described as a group of people who come together to live in a particular area because they have something in common. It is a place in which all aspects of life are drawn together in hope of creating a better way of life for its inhabitants. Each person tends to know everyone else within the community.

In rural communities relationships become friendly and social. Within its boundaries, members must have basic services which are needed to meet their individual and collective needs. There must be agencies of transportation and communication, trade and commerce, and also, education and recreation. "A community is also a feeling. Unless members feel that they belong to one another in a distinctive way, they do not possess a community."[2]

Rural has a very specific meaning in terms of the United States Census. It refers to people living in population divisions of less than 2,000 persons which are not adjacent to or in a continuous development with a city of 5,000 or more people.[3] There may have been a time when urban, suburban, small town, and rural would at least identify basic characteristics shared by a majority of the people living in these areas. This, however, is not true at any level of a society today. If the rural church is to be identified as a community church, it must be located within strategic areas. Of course, the type of church and breadth of the communities served will be the determining factor of its location. As our world has become broadly diverse and complex, so has the rural community.

CHAPTER 1

Ministering in the Highways and Hedges

And the master said to the servant, Go out to the highways and hedges, and compel people to come in, that my house may be filled.
— LUKE 14:23

The underlying motif of this book can best be expressed in these words from the twenty-third verse of the fourteenth chapter of the book of Luke.

In almost every area of the world you will find a rural church: a quaint white frame building nestled in a quiet little town, a Gothic structure with a steeple on an almost deserted street, a storefront in a distant shopping center, or a congregation in a living room of a minister's home.

The rural church serves sparse, small settled areas, but also people who have moved into a nearby small town or city that prefer to return to the "old home church" for worship and other church activities.

In the familiar passage of (Matthew 16:13-18), Jesus promised to build His Church "upon this rock." The Greek word for Peter in this passage is *petros,* which means "a piece of rock" (literally or figuratively). The foundational rock is Jesus. The Church is built upon the identity, person, and mission of Jesus.

The "rock" is generally viewed by many Protestants as Peter's declaration of faith as he spoke for the apostolic band and discerned the true identity of Jesus. By "on this rock" Jesus was saying, "on the solid foundation of faith in me will I erect my edifice in the people of God." By this careful teaching and example, Jesus had developed the faith of this group of men. Once Jesus had ascended to heaven and sent back the Holy Ghost to Peter and all those assembled in the upper room, the promised Church was then built.

There are several words in this book that are used synonymously to designate the people or place of worship in the rural community such as: rural church, local church, old home church, and congregation. These people share similar religious beliefs and are intentionally organized within the religious institution for the express purpose of pursuing the goals and participating in the rites and activities associated with the rural church and community.

The term Church (capitalized), except when modified by a denominational title, refers to the mystical body of people in all ages and all denominations that have attached the Christian name. Literature reveals that the word church is derived from the Greek *kyriake* (belonging to the Lord) and *ecclesia* (an assembly, or gathering). *Ecclesia* in the New Testament is sometimes referred to as the universal church (called out of the world as a whole), but over one hundred times in the Book of Acts of the Apostles and the Epistles, the word describes a rural or local congregation of Christians. They may have had multiple places ("house to house"), but they all were one Church. "In the primary sense, the Church is the worshiping assembly called out by God."

Ecclesia had been used in the Septuagint translation of the Old Testament to describe the congregation of Israel gathering before the Tabernacle in the wilderness. Otherwise, the word was a secular word used mostly in politics, such as to designate a town meeting (Acts 19:32; 39-41). The original *ecclesia* was the citywide Athenian voting constituency. When the City of Athens replaced the old monarchy and aristocracy by creating a democracy, (under Solon, c. 594 BC), and (Clesisthenes, c. 507 BC), they created an *"ecclesia,"* a call for the free citizens of the city to gather and vote. This Athenian *ecclesia,* had the final say on all proposed legislation and judicial appeals (especially on banishing a citizen from the city); it declared war, received ambassadors, elected top city officials and generals (lesser officials were chosen by lot).

The second time Jesus used the word "church" (Matthew 18:17), it was a classical application of the Athenian *ecclesia*.[4] By design, the *ecclesia* (and all its committees, including the council of 500) was citywide and especially precluded any division by neighborhood, family, class, social or economic level, race, or ethnic group.

The Christian Church has generally dated itself from the Day of Pentecost, when a group numbering about one hundred and twenty believers were all filled with the Holy Ghost and began to speak in other tongues as the Spirit gave them utterance (Acts 2:2-4).

The Christian Church as we know it today is a New Testament idea. In the New Testament, the word church appears about 112 times and does not appear at all in the Old Testament. The Church was predestined from before the foundation of world. It was the whole purpose of creation and the central focus of the whole plan of God (Ephesians 1 and 2). The Church is also a select group of individuals who have given their hearts to God and have decided to live according to the principles of His Word.

The Church was purchased with the blood of Jesus. Every Christian was bought and paid for by the blood of Jesus Christ. Thought they have been purchased by God and belong to Him, the people of God have been placed in the care of a minister. As their overseer, a minister has to give an account to God for how he discharges his responsibilities to God and His people (Romans 14:12; Hebrews 13:7).

The Church as the body of Christ was one of the Apostle Paul's favorite ways of describing the Church. Paul employed this figure of speech in writing his letters to the churches at Rome (Romans 12:5), Corinth (1 Corinthians 10:17), Ephesus (Ephesians 1:23), and Colossae (Colossians 1:18). Not only is the Church the body of Christ and God's building, but it is also the bride of Christ.

Jesus is the head of the Church, the body. The people are the members of His corporate body: His hands, His feet, His eyes, and His ears. It is the Church that does the work of God, that preaches, and reaches out to the lost (Ephesians 4:15-16; 5:30; Colossians 1:18; Romans 12:4-5; 1 Corinthians 12:12-27).

The Lord likens the people of His Church to sheep; the Lord is the Great Shepherd and the ministers are the under shepherds who serve under the Chief Shepherd. "To survive, a sheep must always be in a flock, and it must have a shepherd."[5] According to (John 10:1-16; 21:15-17; Matthew 18:12-14; and Luke 12:32) there is no such thing as a "wild sheep."

Each Christian is a temple of the Holy Ghost. In the Old Testament, the Temple in the wilderness and the Temple in Jerusalem served as the house of God. In the New Testament time, the Church is the dwelling place of God's Spirit. Each member of the body of Christ is a part of the "building" (1 Corinthians 3:9-17; 6:19-20;

2 Corinthians 6:6-16; Ephesians 2:19-22; 2 Timothy 2: 20-21; Hebrews 3:1-6; 1 Peter 2:5).

The Church is comprised of all the people of God who have been called out of sin into the glorious kingdom of God. It is a chosen, holy nation of people who have separated themselves from the elements of this world (Romans 1:7; 1 Corinthians 1:2; Ephesians 2:19; and 1 Peter 2:9-10).

The Church universal is a spiritual family, and every church whether small or large, rural or suburban, Apostolic or Catholic, is included.[6] In the new birth experience, the Lord is the Father and the Church is the mother; we are born as children into the family. Our brothers and our sisters in the Lord are often closer to us than certain members of our natural families (Romans 8:14-17; Ephesians 3:15; Galatians 3:26; 4:5-7, 26-31; 1 John 3:1-2).

Religion is a word that many theologians say derived from the Latin *religare,* which means, "to bind,"[7] thus offering an explanation of the general use of the term as a set of beliefs to which the believer is devoted or bound. A rural church is a place or location where religion is practiced.

The Bible is a collection of sacred Scripture comprising 66 books,

> written by many authors, and covering a period of 1600 years. The Old Testament was written mostly in Hebrew (a few short

passages were written in Aramaic). About 100 years before the Christian era, the entire Old Testament was translated into Greek. The New Testament was written in Greek. The Old Testament is comprised of 39 books and the New Testament is comprised of 27 books. Some Bibles (in the Roman Catholic and Orthodox Churches) include the Apocrypha (15 books written in Greek) as part of the Old Testament.[8]

The Bible provides the truth about God and those stories related to God. Men have organized that truth and called it theology. It encompasses the truth about God, Jesus, angels, heaven, hell, death, Satan, and the last days."[9] These are subjects that touch our eternal destinies, both here and in the world to come. Also, the Bible is the authoritative witness to God's revelatory acts through Israel, leading up to His definitive act in Jesus Christ. The Bible contains all that is necessary for salvation and serves to frame the structure of preaching.

The name "Jesus" comes from a Hebrew word meaning "the Lord is salvation." Jesus is the promised Messiah ("Anointed One") who came to save His people from their sins.

Fellowship for the rural church is defined as a group of people voluntarily associated with and joined to one another by reason of their sharing a common religious faith.

Theology is the science or study of God.[10] It is a term compounded of two Greek words, *theos* (God) and *logos* (rational utterance), and it might be taken to mean "rational utterance, or discourse about God, or gods."[11]

In traditional terminology, theology is divided into the following branches:

Biblical Theology. This covers the doctrines of the Bible as well as the disciplines ancillary to their study.

Dogmatic Theology. Dogma is the body of doctrine that has been approved by the Christian Church. It is concerned with the distinctive Christian doctrines of the Trinity, the Incarnation, the Atonement, the Church, the sacraments, and the Last Things.

Symbolic Theology. In practice, this may be regarded as equivalent to dogmatic theology is concerned with credal documents ecumenically received.

Moral Theology. This sometime is known as Christian ethics, treats of Christian conduct. Casuistry is that part of moral theology concerned with problems of conduct and the principles involved in their solution.

Pastoral Theology. In defining pastoral theology we have to preserve the distinction between theology and religion. If we define pastoral theology as the cure of souls, we are, contrary to this distinction, identifying a branch of theology with an activity of religion. Accordingly pastoral theology is concerned with those beliefs and assumptions that lie behind the practice of the cure of souls. Pastoral theology may be associated ascetical theology. This is the theology of the education or training of the soul and differs from pastoral theology only in the greater stress on the element of discipline or self-discipline.

Mystical Theology. This is the theology of the intercourse of the soul with God.

Liturgical Theology. This is the theology of worship.

Philosophical Theology. This treats the philosophical treatment of reality on the assumption that God is part of reality.

Other Divisions. While canon law is not properly a branch of theology it has a theological basis that may be said to constitute its theology.

Certain studies such as Church history and patristic are included under theology but they are not theological. They serve the ends of theology, in particular the history of doctrines and the study of doctrinal texts.[12] However, in modern times, theology has become a generic term for the study of a wider variety of subjects for example, Old Testament, New Testament, church history, ethics, and philosophy of religion.

Prayer is the "approach of human being to God."[13] It can involve intercession, confession, praise, adoration, and thanksgiving, for God alone is worthy to be worshiped. Prayer can include confession of sin, for before

God sinners stand guilty. Also, prayer can involve petition, that is, asking God for personal needs and intercession, asking God for the needs of others. Prayer then is an act to be learned, and so Jesus provides the model for prayer in Matthew 6:9ff. Sometimes prayer is classified in stages, for example, discursive (arising from meditation), effective (arising from experienced meditation), and contemplative (arising from a deep sense of union in love with God).

The term apostle almost without exception is used in the New Testament in a very distinct sense. Generally, the word refers primarily to the twelve men Jesus called out of the larger group of disciples and named them apostles (Luke 6:13; Matthew 10:1-4). The Greek word *apostolos* means literally a delegate, a messenger or "one sent forth"[14] with orders.

Servanthood refers more to an attitude than to specific actions. This was the style of life modeled by Jesus. The servant serves because he wants to do what is best for others.

Preaching is the integral and central function of the rural church and more especially of the ordained ministry. The commission to preach the Gospel is written in almost all ordination rites. It is commanded by Jesus, "Go into all the world and preach the Gospel to the creation" (Mark 16:15), and reinforced by the Apostle Paul when he asked, "how can they believe if they have not heard the message? And how can the message be proclaimed if the message is not sent out?" (Romans 10:14-15).

Preaching for the primitive church was to address those who were not Christians with the Good News of Jesus' death, burial, and resurrection so that they could have an opportunity to believe on His name. Today, preaching is more often that which is done within the Christian congregation. The delivery of a sermon is usually in a service of worship. "The major means of leading people to understand and encounter God's call is preaching."[15]

In the rural church and community, I am aware that there are those who have rejected preaching as having any real or significant influence on the lives of people. However, it may be true that in the past ministers tended to clothe the spoken word in the pulpit with an almost magical aura which is unrealistic. On the other hand, I am convinced that the spoken word does carry much weight and have an influence on the lives of the people of God especially if there are elements of teaching in it.

Books on preaching classify sermons as: expository, thematic, exhortative, and evangelistic. For Protestantism, preaching has always been seen as a means of God's grace: this is why a minister or clergyman is often called "a preacher." The rural church minister who is not equipped to teach the people of God is like a soldier who is trained to meet only half the situations and opportunities that are likely to arise in the course of the battle. The minister stands a good chance of failing, burning out, or leaving the ministry.

A sermon is an address or homily as part of an act of worship. The Eucharist (the Lord's Supper), is normally based on the reading of the Gospel. The purpose of the sermon is to deepen the commitment to Jesus. This may take various forms, for example: words of rebuke, comfort, faith, and hope.

The Lord's Supper is a sacramental rite instituted by our Lord. It was first instituted by Jesus to show forth an example of commemorating His suffering and death. The twelve disciples were witnesses as narrated in Matthew, Mark, and Luke. When Paul wrote to the Corinthians concerning it, he said that it was given to him by revelation. The Lord's Supper, therefore, is a sacred rite to be carried out by the Christian Church. It cannot be neglected without suffering serious harm and incurring the gravest responsibility.

"And he commanded them to be baptized in the name of the Lord" (Acts 10:48). It is noteworthy that Peter "commanded" them to be baptized. It was not a suggestion of what they might consider doing, but an emphatic declaration of what they needed to do to be saved. The Lord had performed a supernatural act by filling them with His Spirit, and it was appropriate for them to respond by obeying the New Testament command to be baptized in water in the name of Jesus Christ for the remission of their sins.

Baptism in the name of Jesus is apostolic in origin and practice (Acts 2:38; 8:12-17; 10:47-48; 19:1-6). Bible students and scholars agree that the apostles founded and gave direction to the Church of God with Jesus Christ being the chief cornerstone. The apostles' teaching and doctrines are fundamental principles upon which the Church is built.

Jesus taught his disciples the plan of salvation. Following His resurrection, they saw Jesus alive and he opened their understanding. The two men en route to Emmaus had their understanding opened up as Jesus said to them, "Thus it behooved Christ to suffer and to rise from the dead the third day; and that repentance and remission of sin should be preached in his name among all nations, beginning at Jerusalem. And ye are witnesses of these things" (Luke 24:13-47).

According to Acts 2:38, the apostles obeyed the command of Jesus Christ in (Luke 24:46-48). In their obedience to the command of Jesus, the apostles became first in a long line of believers to baptize in the name of Jesus Christ.

Thus, baptizing in the name of Jesus Christ is not only apostolic in origin, but in practice as well. No other mode of baptism is found in the New Testament. For more than one hundred years after Pentecost, believers were baptized only in the name of Jesus Christ, for the remission of sins.

> There is no contradiction between Matthew 28:19; Luke 24:45-48; Mark 16:15-19, and Acts 2:38. The NAME of the Father and of the Son and of the Holy Ghost in Matthew 28:19, and MY NAME in Mark 16:15-18, and HIS NAME in Luke 24:47, all mean the same name, Jesus Christ. In Matthew 28:19, a commission or command is given; in (Acts 2:38), a command is executed. In the former, the apostles were told what to do; in the latter, they did it.[16]

There is no scriptural example of any apostle or disciple using the words "in the name of the Father, and the Son, and the Holy Ghost" while administering baptism. The phrase from Matthew 28:19 was clearly understood by the early church. The Son of God was named Jesus by the angel who foretold His birth (Matthew 1:21; Luke 1:31-32). The Son came in His Father's name (John 5:43). The Holy Ghost was given in the name of Jesus (John 14:26); and is the Spirit of Christ (John 14:16-17; Romans 8:9; 1 Peter 1:11). When one obeys Acts 2:38 and is baptized in the name of Jesus Christ, he has also fulfilled Matthew 28:19. When the administrator of baptism calls only the words "son," "father," or "Holy Ghost" over his candidate, he has called no names!

Baptism in the name of Jesus should be administered to all people who show genuine repentance. Indeed, genuine repentance is the only grounds upon which God will accept a sinner. "A broken and a contrite heart he will not despise" (Psalm 51:17).

It should be kept in mind that not only is baptism for the remission of sins; it is also an outward and visible sign of the grace of the Lord Jesus Christ. Through it we are initiated into the fellowship of His Holy Church, and become partakers of His righteousness and heirs of His life. In baptism, "we put on Christ," confessing that we believe in His life, His death, His burial, and His resurrection. As Paul writes to the Romans, "Know ye not, that so many of us as were baptized into Jesus Christ were baptized into His death? Therefore, as Christ was raised from the dead by the glory of the Father, even so we also should walk in the newness of life" (Romans 6:3-4).

Chapter 2

The Impact of the Rural Church

> *As they went on their way through the cities, they delivered to them for observance the decisions which had been reached by the apostles and elders who were at Jerusalem. So the churches were strengthened in the faith, and they increased in numbers daily.*
> – Acts 16:4-5

The word *ecclesia* was not first identified exclusively with the Christian community. It was not until the admission of the Gentiles that the distinction between the Church and Judaism became acute. Thereafter, the word *ecclesia* was applied to the Christian assembly alone.[17]

A Church is a steward of the Gospel. A Church is not entrusted with the Gospel as something to be treasured and kept for itself. The quickest way for a Church to lose the Gospel is to refuse to share it with others.

We can discover the Church in the Bible, in history, or in an evening meeting. Some believe that in many aspects, the Christian Church is the gift of God. The Church has been able to survive centuries of trials and changes only through God's grace and mercy. Its history expresses God's plan for the whole world.

What is the rural church? There seems to be more confusion among people today about the answer to this question than any other within the Christian community. Some say it is a visible religious organization governed by a hierarchy of officials or boards. For others, the rural church is a caring community in a careless world, giving selflessly even to the point of losing its identify in meeting the needs of others. However, others describe the rural church as a building down the road or a place to hold ceremonies at a critical point in life such as birth, marriage, and death.

Members of the rural church are viewed as being a little odd and the minister speaks a language few can understand. Some will even tell you that the rural church is a social club, a place where useful and worthy activities are held especially on Sundays and other selected occasions. Yes, the rural church is all these, but it is something more. It is the body of the Lord Jesus Christ, of which He is head.

The rural church in America is a mystical body of people in all ages and of all denominations that have accepted, participated and found meaning for their lives in Christianity. It is an organization, a human institution subject to the same forces that shape and influence all human communities. "The rural church has a particular sociological character. It shares a common language, meets natural needs for social fellowship, and cultivates specific loyalties. Out of shared commitment the Church sustains its organizational life and interacts with the world."[18]

The organized church is where people come to do God's work. In rural places, the farmer's field is where he plants his crops and does his work. The field as it relates to the rural church is the place where God's work is done. The rural church, like any other church, is a place where people come to be made whole by its teaching. After being taught, they go out to the highways and hedges to demonstrate that teaching by sharing God's love, "the Good News."

If the rural church is to be powerful for God in the community, it must love God's people, accept them, and forgive them, for "... the prayer of the faith will save the sick man, and the Lord will raise him up; and if he has committed sins, he will be forgiven" (James 5:15). The congregation is the primary unit of the rural church. Its members are related to God through fellowship and have accepted the Lord Jesus Christ as their Savior. "These people covenant together to participate in events that recall and manifest their common interest. They celebrate the benevolence of God's love and mercy and they share this with their neighbors."[19]

One of the greatest tragedies that can happen in any church is for the congregation to be divided. Division comes about because of members who want to have things their own way. The greatest thing that can happen in the Church is to let love rule. "A soft answer turneth away wrath: but grievous words stir up anger" (Proverbs 15:1).

Whatever a Church may be theologically, it strives to be a congregation of the Lord.[20] It is also a group of human beings with names, faces, interests, needs, and aspirations. Peoples have joined themselves together, gained support from one another, and collectively carried on the work of the Lord in the rural church community.

The words used to designate the religious leader are priest, pastor, bishop, preacher, and minister etc. "Priest is derived from the word presbyter or elder."[21] In some primitive churches worship services were conducted by the head of the family, such as the patriarch of the tribe or the king of the nation. The word priest denotes an official position or eldership. The words minister, preacher, bishop, and pastor emphasize the function of the religious leader as one who serves at the altar, or who performs priestly duties. The title denotes the one who is the chief servant of the congregation and gives direction to teaching, and other specialized activities such as, serving communion, performing marriage ceremonies, and burying the dead. "The minister is a proclaimer of the insight and information intended to persuade and change people in certain ways."[22]

There is no way of escaping the role expectation that the congregation has for the rural minister. "Problems may arise when the minister discovers that he and the congregation differ on what he should do or not do. The congregation may expect one thing and the minister may expect another."[23]

The rural minister, like most professionals, tends to think in terms of the specialized function of his ministry (preaching, counseling, etc.). The congregation usually thinks in more rational terms: "he gets along with people so well." "He preaches such inspirational sermons." For effectiveness and survival rural ministers and the congregation need to agree on role expectations.

To look for God's people in rural places, the minister must follow the examples of Jesus when He made it clear in the illustration from nature that a spiritual harvest is the result of good seeds planted in good ground, which is the Word of God.

The rural minister alternately finds himself in the role of a farmer of the soil. As one charged with sowing and reaping from God's glory. He must be knowledgeable in the Scripture, alert to opportunities, sensitive to human needs, be approachable, and above all, be patient.

As one in whom God's Word is sown, the minister must be both reactive to His word and willing to apply it to every area of his life. The rural minister should seek to produce the fruit of Jesus Christ.

The mission of the rural church is one of proclamation of the Word of God to the Church and community. The Church cannot hold itself responsible for failure of the people within its community to accept God's Word. The Church is to proclaim the Word with integrity and persistence. Everything else is secondary.

The rural church fails to fulfill its mission when it assumes that the context in which it ministers is the same everywhere and that the channels of effecting its ministry is eternally valid, or when it does not adequately understand the people of the Church and community and the methods necessary to serve them.

For many years, the rural church congregation was a mysterious entity in the institutional church. It did not solve problems by the usual solutions. "Members of the rural church did not buy into programs as others expected them. Ministerial tenure was all too brief and the Church was frequently a place of clergy burnout. Clergy compensation was usually at a minimum and unmet expectations of the minister's spouse created serious tension and problems within the Church and community."[24]

What is now clear is that much of the mystery surrounding the survival of the rural church is embodied in the learning of the rural social science and evangelism. The rural church ministry's first concern must be to identify the people's needs and not just add names to the Church rolls. However, "the minister should make personal contact with every prospective member and should call on inactive members."[25] If this is achieved, evangelism will be given fresh significance and vitality.

In the parable of the great supper, the master ordered his servants to, "Go out to the highways and hedges, and compel people to come in that my house may be filled" (Luke 14:23). The context is clear, however, that the master is underscoring the fact that those who were originally invited and made excuses lost their chance to get in. "He decided to have the remaining places filled by reluctant outsiders who had to be persuaded to come in." Notice who was invited the second time: not to people like the ones on the guest list, but what some might call the social misfits.[26] "Go out quickly into the streets and lanes of the city, and bring in the poor and the maimed and the blind and the lame" (v. 21).

The rural minister like Jesus must seek to permeate the rural community with the Gospel's value. Through the power of the Holy Spirit, the Good News of Jesus Christ is proclaimed and lived. The Holy Spirit will transform individuals, communities, and their structure, liberating the people from sin and oppression. This witness of life through the Word and Sacrament and by service for justice and peace will initiate a response from people who worship at the rural church and live within the community.

In a survey conducted not long ago it was reported that, "one third of all Americans live in rural areas and under the care of rural ministers. Rural people occupy over ninety percent of the land."[27] It is, therefore, imperative that ministers, church administrators, and the rural community understand their history, milieu, especially the changing rural social context and also the extent to which injustice permeates the relations of its social groups, to the best of its traditions and values, and the way in which God is revealed through it. In light of all this, the community called the Church might be built up and strengthen in it.

Chapter 3

The Search for New Life

> *And he said to them, "Go into all the world and preach the Gospel to the whole creation. He who believes and is baptized will be saved; but he who does not believe will be condemned."*
> – Mark 16:15-16

No greater charge has been commanded to anyone. "When Jesus said to us "go" he gave marching orders to the world's greatest army and planting orders to the world's most formidable phalanx of farmers."[28]

The shortest complete sentence possible is, "Go." Anything shorter would contain one letter, and there is no letter in the alphabet that qualifies as a verb, which a complete sentence must have. Since this is an imperative sentence, the subject, you is implied. Therefore the message is, you go. Go is the ultimatum, a mandate.

The command of the Scripture is quite clear; "Witness everywhere and to every person" (Acts 1:8).

Jerusalem represents our town; Judea represents our state; Samaria represents our neighboring states; the uttermost part of the earth represents neighboring nations and all the world. Jesus said, "The field is the world" (Matthew 13:38).

Jesus commanded us to go and search for new life. "Go therefore and make disciples of all nations..." (Matthew 28:19). Without the announcement of His authority, the Great Commission would have lacked justification or motivation. Under the authority of the rural minister, he can direct divine power from heaven and destroy the work of the adversary. Jesus assured us, "he would be with us always, to the close of the age" (Matthew 28:20).

The rural minister knows that the Great Commission has not changed and neither has God's plan of salvation. "It pleased God through the folly of what we preach to save those who believe" (1 Corinthians 1:21). The call of God to his people is to proclaim the Gospel to the end of the earth. "But how are men to call upon him whom they have not believed? And how are they to believe in him of whom they have never heard? And how are they to hear without a preacher? And how can men preach unless they are sent?" (Romans 10:14-15a).

The search for new life is a responsibility and an awesome privilege for God's people. "But you are a chosen race, a royal priesthood, a holy nation, God's own people, that you may declare the wonderful deeds of Him who called you out of darkness into his marvelous light" (1 Peter 2:9).

Evangelism is a divinely given and divinely led enterprise. It represents the initiative of God in Christ Jesus seeking man. Yet, God uses human instrumentality in the quest. As in all other activities where God and man are in partnership, on the human side, preparation is required. "God supplies the conditions for growing of the crop, but the farmer must prepare and cultivate or till the soil. The results of evangelism are more abundant when thorough preparation has been made."[29]

Evangelism is defined as, "the announcement of Good News."[30] The word does not appear in Scripture. However, the word evangelist, including its plural form occurs three times in the New Testament (Acts 21:8; 2 Timothy 4:5; and Ephesians 4:11). The term evangelism for the rural minister encompasses every effort to declare the Good News of Jesus to people in rural places so that they may understand God's grace and mercy.

Evangelism is the work of the Church, which seeks to bring people into its life, and membership.[31] To evangelize in the rural community, the minister must present Jesus in the power of the Holy Spirit, so that people may come to put their trust in God. Also, they must accept Jesus as their Savior, and serve him as their king in the fellowship of His Church.

The fundamental meaning of evangelism is to tell the Good News of Jesus in such a way as to elicit a response of faith and commitment (repenting of sins and being baptized in the name of Jesus Christ and receiving the gift of the Holy Spirit). The heart of evangelism in the rural community is the initial act of confronting someone about Jesus Christ. Jesus said, "For God sent the Son into the world, not to condemn the world, but that the world might be saved through Him" (John 3:17). The most crucial element in evangelism remains the quality of the life experienced in the congregation. "Once people get in the Church, keeping them is the next job."[32]

The evangelism of unbelievers and restoration of the unchurched community members over the years has become a primary concern within the rural church. Some denominations are returning to mass evangelism, while others are turning toward one-on-one evangelism. Rural ministers want an evangelism that not only converts people, but also brings them into the full life of the Church and keeps them.

Rural ministers will agree that evangelism is the practice of the proclamation of the Gospel of Jesus Christ. It is the sharing of glad tidings through Jesus Christ. The Gospel is available on terms which anyone can meet. Evangelism is more than winning those without; it is making the Good News or the Gospel known to and believed by those within the rural church and community.

The Gospel challenges people to transform their lives. It causes them to change and gives them a sense of meaning for living their lives in an extraordinary manner. It will lead them to a deeper commitment to their baptismal promises. People become more and more aware of what it means to belong to the family of God.

It is a high honor and privilege for rural ministers to participate in the mission of Jesus Christ as Priest, Prophet, and King. The minister and the members of the rural church together must keep alive the hopes and dreams of those who have a burning desire to do the will of God. The will of God is that His children become one in Him as they are united with one another. "No program of outreach will work if people are asked to join a Church that does not demonstrate a genuine commitment to Jesus Christ."[33] Those who have repented and believe that Jesus can keep that which He has saved is Good News.

Quite often, the rural minister will quote these Scriptures: "My sheep hear my voice, and I know them, and they follow me; and I give them eternal life, and they shall never perish, and no one shall snatch them out of my hand" (John 10:27-28). "I am the resurrection and life; he who believes in me though he dies, yet shall he live, and whosoever lives and believes in me shall never die" (John 11:25-26). "Peace I leave with you; my peace I give you; not as the world do I give you. Let not your hearts be troubled, neither let them be afraid" (John 14:27).

The Apostle Paul triumphantly claimed this Good News when he declared, "I know whom I have believed, and I am sure that He is able to guard until that day what has been entrusted to me" (2 Timothy 2:12). There seems to be always these two aspects of the Gospel, the Good News that Jesus saves and the Good News that He keeps those He has saved.

Armstrong points out in his book that, "evangelist is not an office that a person holds such as being the head of staff or chair of a board within the Church. It is rather a matter of perspective and style. It is a way of relating to people, a concept of how one fulfill the various roles of a ministry."[34] The rural minister has a responsibility under God that must be carried out. He must be the spearhead for what God is doing in the rural church and in the community.

Rural ministers can learn much from the Apostle's Paul style of ministry and evangelism. Scripture tells us that the apostle "was not ashamed of the Gospel: it is the power of God for salvation to every one who has faith..." (Romans 1:16). Paul knew that the power was in the name of Jesus Christ and not in his own eloquence or wisdom (1 Corinthians 1:17). He resolved, "to know nothing among the people except Jesus and Him crucified" (1 Corinthians 2:2).

Also, the rural minister can learn by looking at the different styles of the apostles and others in their personal encounter with people in various places or situations. A closer look will reveal that to minister to human needs, as Peter and John ministered to the lame beggar at the temple gate, calls for a personal relationship with Jesus (Acts 3:1-10).

Jesus set the example for us, He related to people where they were, while seeing what they could be and at the same time holding up to the people the possibilities of a new life. Jesus invited, but He did not insist. He challenged, but He did not coerce. He also condemned sin, yet He did not condemn the repentant sinner (John 8:1-11).

If the rural minister will take a closer look at Jesus, he would see that "He never neglected man's need for reconciliation with God. He crossed all barriers of race, cultures, economic situations to bring healing to man's pain. Jesus stood against everything which threatened the freedom and integrity of men."[35]

Any number of rural ministers will tell you that evangelism is the proclamation of the historical Jesus as Savior and God, to persuade men, women, boys, and girls to come to Jesus and be saved from their sins. Ephesians 4:11 points out that the Apostle Paul declared that Jesus gives gifts to men, "and His gifts were that some shall be apostles, some prophets, some evangelists, some pastors and teachers." These are commonly referred to as "the fivefold ministry gifts."

The Bible indicates that the gift of the evangelist is just as important for the Church today as it was for the early Church. In Acts 21:8 Phillip is called an evangelist;

and in 2 Timothy 4:5 he is charged to "do the work of an evangelist."

As rural ministers struggle with the insurmountable problems within the Church and community, the unrest, and problems garner around the world. This situation simply accentuates the message of the one who proclaimed, "I am the light of the world; he who follow me will never walk in darkness, but will have the light of life" (John 8:12). Jesus is the promised Messiah of Israel. He is the hope of the Gentiles which includes most of the world's population, whether they are Asian, African, American, or European.

In my tenure as a minister in the rural church and community, I have found that most unchurched people have a "come and get me attitude." Although residents are interested in the Church and will respond to pastoral visits, still only a few take the initiative to come to Church on a regular basis. This is a prominent characteristic of rural unchurched people. The rural church is compelled to go to people via cultivation and personal visitation.

The rural minister must insure, by all means, that the community is welcome, wanted, needed and will be allowed to participate in the activities of the Church. In spite of this, religious polls reveal that most rural residents are interested in the Church and its programs. However, fellowship cultivation is needed to galvanize people into a participation mode. Just as any other type of Church, or its location, the rural church is also expected to go to the community and witness to the people. Members within the community expect to be found and asked to become a part of the Church. Yet, they will do little to hasten or facilitate the process. The rural church will get the people that it persistently cultivates or goes after when they demonstrate the love of Christ to them.

No rural minister can have the Lord's blessing on his ministry until he realizes that he must totally depend on Jesus.[36] The fire of the Holy Spirit will produce a burning heart and a vision to fulfill the Lord's command to do his will. A burning heart will ultimately result in a powerful ministry. The rural minister that is not anointed by the Holy Spirit will not weather the storm, especially in the rural church. "The ministers who evidence the anointing of the Holy Spirit are those who remain perpetually fresh in their message and outlook."[37] If the rural minister's message is anointed by the Holy Spirit, it will be delivered with authority.

Jesus challenges us to transform our lives (Romans 12:2). "Energized by the Holy Spirit, we began to live our ordinary lives in an extraordinary manner."[38] Jesus leads us to a deeper commitment and awareness of His blessings and promises. We become more aware of what it means to belong to God's family. The will of the Lord simply is that we be one in Him as we are united with one another. Together, we walk in faith while we search for new life.

CHAPTER 4

Life in the Rural Church and Community

And many people will come and say: "Come let us go to the mountain of the Lord, to the house of the God of Jacob; that He may teach us His ways and that we may walk in His paths." For out of Zion shall go forth the law, and the word of the Lord from Jerusalem.
— Isaiah 2:3; Micah 4:2

Rural churches of every size, small or large, are called to be communities of faith. They must participate in the continuing ministry and mission of the Lord, in ways appropriate to size, resources, and location. The Church is called to embody its members in the corporate life of the Church, and demonstrate the love of God to the end that people and social structures are transformed toward personal wholeness, social justice, and good stewardship.

In the rural church, members must recognize and emphasize the positive aspect of size in order to overcome the defeatism that to be small is somehow inadequate. The rural religious community has been affected by this secular attitude.

The majority of the rural churches in America remain small. Research by Lyle Schaller and others have revealed that,

> fifty percent of the churches in the United States have fewer than seventy-five persons in attendance at the weekly worship services; seventy-five percent have fewer than one hundred and forty persons in attendance. These small and middle size congregations are typical sizes in America. Only five percent of the churches in America average more than three hundred persons in attendance for the weekly services.[39]

Church programs must be attractive and motivating in order to hold people and encourage them to attend regularly and to participate in the worship experience.

In rural areas, more members of the Church seek an authentic personal experience and a closer interpersonal relationship with God and each other. The mission of the rural church, whether small or large, is the same. The Church is the people of God called out to grow in grace, to be in the world to minister, and to serve in love.

People are often judged in rural communities by the kind of work they do for a living, the area in which they live, and the kind of automobile they drive. The members of the community having highly visible positions or having professions that require multiple degrees such as physicians, attorneys, college professors, and teachers, seem to get more attention; while people doing menial jobs are considered less important. "Certainly for the Christian this way of judging people is not proper; for worth is found in our being in God's image, not in our function within a society."[40]

Regrettably, this criterion for evaluation of a person's worth is also found in the rural church.

> Members who have highly visible or important positions, such as ministers, evangelists, deacons, ministers of music, and those persons chairing committees, are looked upon with favor; while others who are involved with less visible positions are often ignored or looked down on.[41]

The Bible tells us that, "he has put down the mighty from their thrones, and has exalted those of low degree; He has filled the hungry with good things, and the rich He has sent empty away" (Luke 1:52-53). The rural church of today must never subscribe to the theory that, "if they are not like us they cannot be a part of us."[42] For Christians, all occupations, vocations, and positions in the rural church are equally honorable if one is fulfilling God's will. The most esteemed positions, however, are not to be sought after if they are not in God's will. Submission to God is of the utmost importance.

Life in the rural church involves witnessing that calls its members to a personal commitment to Jesus Christ as Lord and Savior. The Church is composed of members with many skills, interests, and abilities. All these skills can be used in meeting the needs of the people, both within the rural church and within the community.

Small rural churches may be somewhat analogous to the extended family. "It is a group that continues over time in some cases for a lifetime. It has heritage that gives members a sense of identity, of knowing who they are. It celebrates members victories and supports them in times of difficulty."[43] At times there may be internal tension and conflict, but it closes rank when any member is threatened by external forces.

The rural church can be caring and loving, but it can and sometimes does discipline members who deviate from its norm. "Many people value the Church as a place to meet people. Deep friendships are made and maintained in churches"[44] although there are other places where the community is nourished. One of the primary reasons that people seek out the Church is to find congenial people and to enjoy their company. One older member of a rural church was overheard saying recently:

> I really get a lot out of it. Well, companionship for one thing... belonging. I think that's very important, especially nowadays when you can't even visit your friends without a written invitation, because everybody's so wrapped up in their own tiny world, and they don't want you butting in. So it's very hard to really belong anywhere except to your own family. And I think in a church you have a feeling of belonging and being with other people that feel the same way you do about things. And it's a very good feeling.[45]

A person cannot join a family, he must be adopted. The same is true of the rural church. Individuals do no just join the rural church, they are adopted. Once received into the family, members become an integral part of it and share the rights and obligations of the congregation. The faithfulness of its members provides inspiration and emotional warmth to the Church and community.

An outstanding characteristic of the rural church is that it functions like a family. It has a kind of mutual sympathy, trust and forgiveness among it members that will enable them to know, perhaps for the first time, what it is like to be in a church where members are loved in spite of all their weaknesses and faults. They are loved just because they are children of God.

In the rural church and community, people are seldom rejected because they get in trouble with the law, wear second hand clothing, or talk too much. Members are taught to help one another, to associate with one another, and criticize one another only in love (1 Peter 1:22).

The family relationship is not sentimental. However, it involves the kind of sympathy that come from knowing that no matter how weak another may be you do not have to stoop down to help him, because your weaknesses have put you there alongside him already. The Apostle Paul tell us, "We who are strong ought to bear with the failing of the weak, and not to please ourselves; let each of us please his neighbor for his good, to edify him" (Romans 15:1-2). Maybe this is why Apostle Peter became such an inspiring leader of the early church. He was never able to look down on any man but only stand with men in sympathy, knowing that he himself had denied Jesus three times, (Acts 3:3-7; John 18:27).

The role of the minister in the rural church is to equip members so that they may grow in the "discipline and instruction of the Lord" (Ephesians 6:4; 1 Thessalonians 2:11). He must foster personal, spiritual, social, political, and economical changes for all age groups. The minister must help the rural church and community to solve its problems. The rural minister must help the people to form partnerships and network with religious and nonreligious organizations that address social issues relative to the rural church and community.

Life in the rural church exists for these reasons:

- *Koinonia* – The Greek word for fellowship, communion: e.g., the fellowship of the Holy Spirit (2 Corinthians 13:14);
- *Didache* – To develop and nurture the religious traditions that they received and pass them on to the succeeding generations;
- *Kerygma* – To be a base for sharing the faith with outsiders;
- *Diakonia* – To prepare members for service in the world.[46]

These are some of the powerful tools that the rural church may use to communicate to the community:

A. The newsletter is one of the best forms of communication because it can reach people who may not come to Church on a regular basis. It can be any size or length, produced weekly, monthly, or quarterly. It can include such things as the Church calendar or events, summaries of committees meetings, notes for members, profiles of new members, birth announcements, news from local, state, and national conventions. The newsletter can include news from special groups (women, men, youth, etc.), needs of the Church members, and an inspirational section.

B. The Church bulletins are given to those who attend service on Sunday mornings, but unless they are mailed or taken to those who are absent from service, especially the sick and shut-in, they will reach only those who attend service. In addition to the order of service, the bulletins usually contain a calendar of events, announcements, prayer requests, and news about the rural church family and community.

C. Information tables in the church can display the latest magazines and material for devotion, books, tracks, and brochures.

D. The local newspaper is one of the best communication tool available. Most local newspapers have a special section for religious opportunities. The information is printed free of charge in most cases. Keep in mind that the message must be short and precise.

E. Local radio stations like the newspaper will air short messages free of charge. Again, the messages must be short and to the point.

F. The telephone may be employed when the community is large. The telephone is especially good when there is a need to notify the Church family of a serious illness, emergencies, or to urge the congregation to attend a special meeting.

To make known your message about the rural church and community is a lot of work; however, it can be very rewarding. The relationship between the Church and community must be one of mutual benefit and commitment.

The rural church brings stability to families. The Church and community draw strength from each other. The Church provides a model for marital love, for marriage is a type of relationship between the Lord Jesus Christ and His Church. "People should come to know the Church for its positive influences community and also for its leadership in practical matters."[47] There should be adequate parking for automobiles so that people who attend church do not have to park in the street, narrow roads, or on private property near the Church.

The rural church can also provide excellent community services such as day care for little children, drug and alcohol counseling and related services. These things make the rural church vulnerable to many problems, but they also will contribute to a positive image. The rural church is a place where people can find answers to their problems, questions, and prayers. "The rural pastor must accept the people for what they are and for what they can become. He can use their gifts and talents to make life in the rural church and community a better place to work, worship, live, and raise a family."[48]

Worship is not limited to what we sing or what we say in our prayers. Worship is better identified through our priorities. We worship what we serve and what we make preeminent in our lives (Romans 1:21-22; Titus 3:3). Whatever is preeminent in our lives is indeed what we worship.

CHAPTER 5

The Importance of Pastoral Counseling

Brethren, if a man is taken in any trespass, you who are spiritual should restore him in a spirit of gentleness. Look to yourself, lest you too be tempted. Bear one another's burdens, and so fulfill the law of Christ.
— GALATIANS 6:1-2

The counseling ministry in the rural church is the most misunderstood of all the ministries. It has never been more evident than it is now. People need godly counseling to proceed confidently through life. The teaching in Holy Scripture to seek counseling is clear, "The wise man also may hear and increase in learning, and the man of understanding acquire skill" (Proverbs 1:5; 9:9). Counseling is not a pastoral specialty in most cases. However, it is a vital element of almost every pastoral function. A rural minister does not hold special office hours to perform the duties of a counselor. "The rural minister is always counseling in one way or another, in everything he does. The less he advertises himself as a counselor, the better counselor he becomes."[49]

For eternal success, counseling must be done within the spiritual and moral teaching guidelines of the Bible regardless of the counselor's professional identification, social or religious role, or area of expertise. The minister's counseling becomes pastoral when the counselee or counselor focuses the relationship upon the relation of God to the process of their lives.

According to Holman Bible Dictionary, "a counselor is one who analyzes a situation and gives advice to one who has responsibility for making a decision."[50] The Hebrew word translated counselor in Isaiah 9:6 is *ya'ats,* which means to advise: to deliberate or resolve. "Counseling is a service designed to help people arrive at wise choices and adjustments in connection with problems and options in their lives."[51] "Every person who expresses the desire to talk, therefore, is really looking for a support or an enlightenment."[52] The pastoral counselor must see the ministry of counseling as both an achievement and a gift, personal discipline and spontaneous to the call of Jesus Christ.

In reality, "counseling is a nonmedical discipline. The aim of counseling is to facilitate and encourage personality growth and development. It helps persons to modify areas in their lives which have become problems. Also, it provide inspiration and wisdom for persons facing the inevitable losses and disappointments in life."[53] The pastoral counselor's duty or task is to heal, to remedy often, and to comfort always. "Persons who seek pastoral counseling sometimes suffer from interpersonal conflicts."[54] People in this category feel the need to talk with the minister of the Church because they feel he is competent and more experienced than other ministers within the rural church. The pastoral counselor must provide both objectivity and a reasonable degree of privacy for those persons who seek this kind of service.

The counseling ministry in the rural church should be performed under the supervision of the minister if not performed by him. Those counselors who serve under the minister should be spiritually oriented and utilize spiritual methods in helping people to solve their problems. They should place more faith in the ministration of God's power than upon their own abilities or upon psychological methods. Counseling in the rural church setting should take cognizance of the counselee's spiritual nature and needs. Psychological techniques may serve a useful purpose in aiding the religious counselor as he ministers to the many aspects of the congregational needs within the rural church and community.

The rural minister uses various methods in helping the people that come to him for counseling. Pastoral counselors eagerly accept the resources of psychology, psychiatry, and social work. In general, they see these resources as additional tools to enhance but not to replace prayer, Scripture, and various religious oriented activities.

One of the common phrases in the New Testament is, "the deceitfulness of the flesh" (Galatians 5:17; 2 Peter 2:10). This implies that people are blind and do not know what is wrong. One of the tremendous joys of rural ministry is "turning on the lights" for people. The Bible tells us that, "The unfolding of thy words gives light: it imparts understanding to the simple" (Psalm 119:130).

Having spiritual as well as psychological tools may make the pastoral counselor more effective; however, his task is sure to be somewhat easier. With every new tool comes the challenge of how it should be used. A new decision must be made for each person who comes with a unique problem. "Pastoral counselors usually have a strong motivation for study and self-improvement. They must learn to use judiciously both spiritual and psychological tools to accomplish their missions."[55]

Almost every family magazine or newspaper carries a column or article on counseling, marriage problems, childcare, or some other area of human problems. "Television and movies have capitalized on public interest in human problem solution."[56] The role of the counselor, particularly the psychiatrist, has been glamorized and forced upon an awakened and sensitive public in the much-watched soap operas.

Journalists and those who promote the entertainment media know how to present their cure for human problems for those who may have personal difficulties. Readers and viewers may identify with either the counselee or the counselor. Through vicarious experiences they are entertained, educated, and possibly helped. Also, the very humaneness of man turns his attention toward his troubled neighbor.

Only the very naive would believe that the counseling episodes depicted in the mass communication media are beneficial. Without denying the humanitarian impulses of those impulses of those who publish and produce, it is likely that their primary objectives are larger subscriptions and higher ratings for entertainment values and appeal. While some educational values may evolve, much of the material of this type presents faulty information. However, there are exceptions to any rule.

The broadening interest in the counseling profession by the rural church and community has urged ministers to get certified or at least some training in pastoral counseling. This desire by rural ministers to seek training in pastoral counseling theories and techniques have superseded the capacities of the limited training facilities in the universities, seminaries, and bible schools. As a result of these factors, charlatans who set up counseling practices in rural communities under the guise of professionals are attempting things beyond their capacities.

The question is, who should counsel in rural communities? The consideration of who should counsel is a weighty question. One segment of community critics says that counseling belongs only to persons who are professionally trained. Still, others will tell you that the minister of the rural church should do the counseling. However, "it is wrong to allow incompetent practitioners to deal with problems which may be made worse by improper counseling, no matter how well the intention of the counselor may be."[57]

The rural minister should realize that preaching is only one method of helping people face their problems and to live as Christians. "The minister should not attempt to do in the pulpit what should be done in pastoral counseling or perhaps in a series of counseling sessions. Some problems can only be dealt with face to face where the counselee has the opportunity to express himself, ask questions, and to relieve tension."[58] Preaching can never take the place of pastoral counseling or pastoral care.

Many churches in rural communities in America expect their pastor to fulfill all the religious objectives of a church body composed of hundreds of members. Even in a small rural church, a minister cannot attend to every detail of the Church. Some objectives, regardless of the size of the Church, must be delegated to other qualified members. Smaller churches must be adequately staffed in the same way as the larger churches when there are qualified members in the congregation.

In the past, many denominations have been content to assist new members in their search for a closer relationship with God only to leave them to fend for themselves. "Few, if any, religious groups ignore completely the physical and psychological needs of its members today."[59] The rural church in America should pledge its concerns and constant efforts to assist not only its own members, but also the community at large to become happier and better adjusted children of God.

Time available to the rural minister must be divided in many ways. As the congregation grows larger, his work becomes more difficult and demanding. He must have concerns not only with the pulpit task, but also for teaching, evangelism, finance, administration, pastoral counseling, and visitation. Even if some of these tasks are delegated to paid or to volunteered staff, "the pastor is never relieved from any of them."[60]

Regardless of the interest, the minister may not be able to do all the pastoral counseling that should be done, even in small rural churches. There will be some members that will demand the minister's individual attention regardless of the number of other good counselors in the Church. Because of his position and the feelings that members have of their rural minister, he is likely to be called upon for more counseling than he can do.

The rural minister as counselor enters into the Church as one who seeks to mediate the healing and redeeming love of God. "He does not compel, but he does respond. He does not command, but he does guide. He does not manipulate, but he does respect the moving of the Spirit at work within the congregation as he serves as a midwife of ideas and growth in the Lord within each member of the Church."[61] The Lord does not require what is impossible for the rural minister to give or do. All that He wants him to do is, "be faithful."

When a rural minister sees only the present and fails to consider the future, he invites disappointment. Christians need to comprehend that God is good to his people all the time, even when they do not understand Him and mistakenly accuse Him or question His goodness.

Jesus said that love, even for the unlovely, the corrupt, those that need counseling, and for the down and out, was the greatest commandment. Also, that love practiced fulfills all the law. This Jesus practiced continually and the rural minister should do this to.

CHAPTER 6

The Mission of the Rural Church Within the Community

> *I will give you the keys of the kingdom of heaven, and whatever you bind on earth shall be bound in heaven, and whatever you loose on earth shall be loosed in heaven.*
> – MATTHEW 16:19

A basic biblical passage dealing with the origin of the Church is found in (Matthew 16:19). Inherent in the very foundation of the Church is its mission. Christ commissioned has echoed through the world, and transcending time.

There are two primary forms of the Church life: the gathered community and the scattered community. "In many ways the gathered community exist to draw support and resources for the community in its scatteredness to empower the members for their mission within the community."[62]

William Barclay has passed on an account of a man who came to an Indian minister pleading to be allowed to become a member of the Church. "The minister knew that this man had not received any previous instruction or teaching in the faith from the Church. So naturally the minister wanted to be certain that the man knew what he was doing."[63]

"Tell me," he said, "Why are you so anxious to become a member of the Church?"

The man answered: "By chance there came into my hands a copy of Luke's Gospel. I read it and I thought that I had never heard of anyone so wise and wonderful as Jesus, and I wished to take him as my master and my Lord. But at that stage, I thought that it was simply a matter between Him and me and no one else. Then by chance I got a copy of the book of Acts. Here was a difference. Luke was all about what Jesus said and did. But at the end of Luke, Jesus ascends to his Father, and The Acts begins with the same story. In The Acts, Jesus is no more on earth in the flesh. The Acts, is not so much about what He said and did as it is about what Peter and Paul said and did, and above all, about what the Church said and did." So, said the man, "I felt I must become a member of the Church which carries on the life of Jesus Christ."[64] Simply put, this is the mission of the Church: to carry on the life of Jesus Christ in the world.

Jesus came into the world for redemptive purpose. He was to reveal God the Father to man and redeem men from their sin. The responsibility of the rural church is to show God to men and present the redemptive message of Jesus. "The Church was made for mission. When Jesus gathered a group of people who were committed to him, He committed to them a mission."[65]

The commission of Jesus is a mandate with a world scope, all nations, even until the end of the world (Matthew 28:19-20). The mission Jesus describes is the most demanding assignment ever made. Christ, who commissioned His Church and gave His followers their marching orders, describes His work in the world in clear terms. That contemporary challenge is as exciting today as the original one. The rural church must be able to take hold of its mission on Christ's term, teaching the Gospel message to everyone in its community.

The rural church has two broad areas of work. First, the Church must function to build up and strengthen its own body. It must reach out beyond itself, to those in need of the Gospel message. The object of the mission effort is to extend its ministry and witness to persons who are separated from the Church by barriers, which must be crossed.

Second, the rural church is to extend its mission throughout America and the world. This can be done by sending money and or missionaries to areas that need help. "What the Church can do personally in mission work is done through direct action. Direct action is called mission action. What a church cannot do directly, it gets done through representatives."[66]

Jesus said this to His disciples, "Peace be with you. As the Father has sent me, even so I send you" (John 20:21). The rural church exists by mission. The members of the rural community does not have to be too alert to recognize that Satan is working overtime in the churches and communities within America. The rising crime rate, addiction to drugs and alcohol, the change in moral standards, laws and conduct, corporate evils, such as prejudice, poverty, and hunger are pressing priorities. Christians live under the mandate as stated in the twenty-fifth chapter of Matthew, remembering always that as we minister to others, it is a ministry to the Lord Jesus Christ (v. 40).

There are members of the rural church and community in America that "hesitate out of personal insecurity not knowing whether they will stand alone, or if they do, whether they will be strong enough to carry the battle through."[67] The Apostle Paul said, "Let us not grow weary in well doing, for in due season we shall reap, if we do not lose heart" (Galatians 6:9).

Doubt finds its way at one time or another into the life of all Christians. It strikes at the minister as well as the seasoned members, or the new convert. The members of the rural church and community who are faced with doubt do not have to be afraid, for Jesus said, "I will never fail you nor forsake you" (Hebrews 13:5).

The mission of the rural church within the community is the same as it was for John in his days. "John's task was to march boldly into the religious system and proclaim what would be, to the Jews, a shocking new message. It was to be a message of repentance, a turning from the ways of sin in preparation for the coming of the Lord and Savior Jesus Christ" (Luke 3:2-4). The rural minister in America must have the calling and the anointing for mission in the community.

The mission of the rural church within the community is to be friendly. "The minister should enlist those persons who have the gift of hospitality and engage them in an intentional effort to foster and facilitate a pleasant atmosphere by bringing people together."[68]

Friendliness begets friendliness, and it is hoped and expected that members of the rural church and community be gregarious and outgoing. Everything about our lives must be placed in the light of our faith in the Lord Jesus Christ. The command of the Gospel is, "Go out to the highways and hedges, and compel people to come in that the Lord's house may be filled" (Luke 14:23).

Members of the rural church know that it is their responsibility to effect change in their community by giving people what they need rather than leaving them in their present condition. God is ready, the Comforter has come, and hungry hearts will receive His power if the Church will let it flow out from them.

CHAPTER 7

The Significance of Faith

> *Now faith is the assurance of things hoped for, the conviction of things not seen. For by it men of old received divine approval. By faith we understand that the world was created by the word of God, so that what is seen was made out of things which do not appear.*
> – HEBREWS 11:1-3

The only actual biblical definition of faith (Hebrews 11:1) does not encapsulate all that the Bible says about the subject. But it does indicate the main points: "the assurance of things hoped for, the conviction of things not seen." The centrality of faith for Christians dates from the New Testament. The noun "faith" is comparatively rare in the Old Testament,[69] where in (e.g. Habakkuk 2:5) it may indicate "faithfulness" or "loyalty" to God rather than purely passive reliance. However, dependence on God as distinct from human power was important for Isaiah (Isaiah 7:9; 30:15). The Old Testament so often sees faith concretized as obedient action (Deuteronomy 6:11 ff., etc.), the note of trust also resounds, especially in the Psalms.[70]

Everyone's experience and relationship with God starts with faith. Faith is the foundation of everything that we receive from God. "For by the grace given to me I bid every one among you not to think of himself more highly than he ought to think, but to think with sober judgment, each according to the measure of faith which God has assigned him" (Romans 12:3).

Since God dealt us the measure of faith, what we do with it and how we develop it is all important. There is an old adage which says, "The longest journey begins with a single step." "Where the journey of faith eventually takes us depends on how much or how little we are able or willing to utilize our faith."[71] The Scripture goes on to let us know that, "Without faith it is impossible to please Him. For whoever would draw near to God must believe that He exists and that He rewards those who seek Him" (Hebrews 11:6).

Faith is not the product of an emotional tangent that influences our passion only for a short time. Many valuable experiences, both natural and spiritual, have been attained by faith in the rural church and community in America. Faith brings into the realm of possibility things that would be impossible to attain by any other means.

Abraham knew a son by Sarah was impossible due to her age. He was a hundred years old, and Sarah was over ninety. Also, she had never been able to conceive a child before. I do not think Abraham was ignoring those facts. But God made the difference. "With God all things are possible" (Matthew 19:26).

"Without weakening in his faith, Abraham faced the fact that he and Sarah were past the time of producing a child. Yet he did not waver through unbelief regarding the promises of God, but was strengthened in his faith and gave God the glory, being fully persuaded that God had power to do what He had promised" (Romans 4:19-21). "Faith that ignores fact misses the point"[72] (but it sounds like it is the point). Jesus said that faith is very much like a small seed. "It doesn't take much faith to do wonderful and powerful things."[73]

"Faith, in its very nature, demands action. Faith can be tested by action. The Bible informs us with such inspiring illustrations of men and women whose faith in God was obvious from their actions and decisions."[74] "Rahab is listed in Hebrews as having faith when she welcomed the Israelite spies into her home. She allied herself with God's people. Joseph literally gave the empty coat to Potiphar's wife to avoid immorality. Moses abandoned the pleasure and privileges of a son of Pharaoh to identify himself with the afflicted people of God. Elijah boldly challenged the prophets of Baal to a sacrificial contest saying, "The God who answers by fire, let him be God." Then with apparent brashness,

Elijah proceeded to dump jars of water on the sacrifices. Elijah knew his living, powerful God would reply, and He did. Beaten and imprisoned, Paul and Silas prayed and sang hymns of praise to God at midnight" (Hebrews 11). "These were not simply pious expressions but confessions and acts of faith from men and women who had enough faith to trust God."[75]

The significance of faith is that it inspires us to pray more fervently, give more, be more faithful, and seek to portray Jesus. "The invisible part of man enters the invisible things of the universe by faith."[76] Faith enlightens us and is the foundation of true understanding. Faith makes known the hope Jesus had in calling us to work for Him.

The possibilities of faith are as vast as God. Faith brings us into the ream of possibility that God can do anything but fail."[77] "God can do all things" (Philippians 4:13). "Life is too complex and unpredictable, too difficult and too severe for us to face it with only our own feeble powers."[78] I believe that having faith in the living God can cause a man to experience the rich blessings of our Lord and Savior Jesus Christ.

A hymn that expresses well the reality of the significance of faith in all of life's situations is based on the promise of Jesus' continuing presence. For He has said, "I will never fail you" (Hebrews 13:5); "And lo, I am with you always, to the close of the age" (Matthew 28:20). As we grasp this promise of Jesus and live in its light, we can share in the life of faith which this writer affirms:

> I take Thy promise, Lord, in all its length,
> And breadth and fullness, as my daily strength,
> Into life's future fearless I may gaze,
> For, Jesus, Thou art with me all the days.
>
> There may be days of darkness and distress,
> When sin has power to tempt, and care to press;
> Yet in the darkest day I will not fear,
> For, 'mid the shadows, Thou wilt still be near.
>
> Days there may be of joy, and deep delight,
> When earth seems fairest, and her skies most bright;
> Then draw me closer to Thee, lest I rest
> Elsewhere, my Savior, than upon Thy breast.
>
> And all the others days that make my life,
> Mark'd by no special joy or grief or strife,
> Days fill'd with quiet duties, trivial care,
> Burdens too small for other hearts to share.
>
> Spend Thou these days with me, all shall be Thine
> So shall the darkest hour with glory shine.
> Then when these earthly years have pass'd away,
> Let me be with Thee in the perfect day.[79]

CHAPTER 8

Preaching in the Rural Church – Two Sermons

> *Preach the word, be urgent in season and out of season, convince, rebuke, and exhort, be unfailing in patience and in teaching. For the time is coming when people will not endure sound teaching, but having itching ears they will accumulate for themselves teachers to suit their own liking, and will turn away from listening to the truth and wander into myths.*
> – 2 Timothy 4:2-4

In the New Testament "preaching" refers to the proclamation of the Gospel to non-Christians. "The first English form of the word preach was *preachen* from the Latin *praedicare* to proclaim, to announce, to declare."[80]

Christian preaching is rooted in the biblical revelation, where it has a three-fold responsibility. It has first to elucidate for the hearers the meaning of the text for those who first wrote it and first heard or read it. "The work of exegesis; it has to translate that meaning into the terms and understanding of the twentieth-century culture: the work of interpretation; it has to relate the meaning of the text to the contemporary situations personal and corporate, which the hearers are confronted."[81]

Preaching in the rural church is usually embodied in a sermon, an ordered discourse which is expected to have a progression of thought with points clearly made in intelligible language, illustrative material, and an attempt to invoke a response from the congregation. The message may contain material from the tradition and experience, past and present, of the Church, and from the minister's own experience.

If preaching could be defined only according to success, our understanding of what preaching is and can be would be severely limited. If our definitions say that preaching occurs only when it is intentional, conscious, or successful—that is, when mutual understanding takes place, we have limited our range of understanding and most likely are ignoring some important aspects of the preaching phenomenon. Whether "message sent" equals "message received" is important, but does not encompass all that needs to be observed and understood about preaching. "Not so good preaching is preaching nevertheless, and often has impact, but it may be quite different from the impact the minister intended."[82]

The French preacher, Jean Claude (whose discourse on The Composition of a Sermon he used), "saw that a sermon should clearly and purely explain a text, recovering the sense it had for the biblical author."[83] Claude, therefore, followed six rules frequently used by biblical scholars to describe the characteristic message of early Christian evangelists. The six rules of Claude are:

1. A preacher should never choose text which he himself does not understand. That is to say, do not isolate one or two words, or phrases, which do not reveal the context of the biblical passage. Remember – you want to preach the intent of the biblical writer, not your own ideas.

2. Exposition must include the complete sense of the writer. It is his language and his sentiments which you ought to explain.

3. Be selective in what text you choose, for you can take too much. By not being selective of those aspects of theology you wish to give your audience, you may loose them.

4. Pay due regard to the context – that is, to the times, place, and persons associated with the text.

5. Do not choose an unusual text out of personal vanity, simply to show yourself off as being

original or clever. Rather, choose a text that is straightforward in expressing some aspect of the truth.

6. Do not censure your audience with a text. But if you do judge your audience, let it be done with wisdom, tempered with sweetness of spirit.[84]

Much of what Jean Claud taught Charles Simeon is now common homiletical practice and is still valuable advice.

The Greek word for proclamation is *kerygma*; this word is frequently used by biblical scholars to describe the characteristic message of early Christian evangelists. It is generally believed this *kerygma* contained the following:

1. A brief outline of Jesus' ministry

2. An account of his birth, death, resurrection, and exaltation

3. A proclamation of his Second Coming, and

4. A call to repentance and an offer of forgiveness of sins and the gift of the Holy Ghost.[85]

The rural minister sees the Book of Acts as much more than just a book of ancient history. It depicts the many and varied aspects of the ministry of the apostles. It is a book that gives a true picture of the Church of Jesus, which reflects the nature and character of Jesus in its dealing with a sin-plagued world shrouded in darkness.

Acts is the defining book of the New Testament. "It defines what it means to be born again and to become a part of the Church. It further defines the purpose of the Church through the preaching and practice of the apostles of Jesus and the early believers as they sought to fulfill the Great Commission, which Jesus gave them prior to His ascension."[86] The book also establishes both by preaching and precedent that which the rural church should expect as it encounters the forces of darkness in its community.

The goal of preaching in the rural church is to "incorporate the congregation into the preach Word, and to give voice to the hopes and fears, victories and defeats that are part of the journey of faith."[87] Those of us who preach take our cue from the Holy Spirit, what we preach is a God given "foolishness." The Apostle Paul's term for it (1 Corinthians 1:21) is not all that can be said about it, but it remains permanently true. The Gospel is a stumbling block to people whose mind is not yet opened to the message of Jesus Christ our Lord and Savior.

Sermon Number One

Feeding The Lambs And Sheep

The text:

As a lily among brambles, so is my love among maidens. As an apple tree among the trees of the woods, so is my beloved among young men. With great

delight I sat in his shadow, and his fruit was sweet to my taste. He brought me to the banqueting house, and his banner over me was love.
— Song of Solomon 2:2-4

When they had finished breakfast, Jesus said to Simon Peter, "Simon, son of John, do you love me more than these?" He said to him, "Yes, Lord; you know that I love you." He said to him, "Feed my lambs." A second time He said to him, "Simon, son of John, do you love me?" He said to Him, "Yes Lord; you know that I love you." He said to him, "Tend my sheep." He said to him the third time, "Simon, son of John, do you love me?" Peter was grieved because He said to him the third time, "Do you love me?" And he said to Him, "Lord, you know everything; you know that I love you." Jesus said to him, "Feed my sheep."
— John 21:15-17

Feeding The Lambs And Sheep

What is love? That is the question. Love is at the heart of our Christian faith. Throughout both the Old Testament and New Testament we are told that love to God and love to our brothers and sisters are the genuine expressions of spiritual and physical growth and development. To be genuinely Christian is to live by the principles of love everyday. In an atmosphere created by love, every child of God can find stimulation and creative encouragement which makes for true fulfillment.

When Jesus spoke of love as being the badge of Christian discipleship (John 13:34-35) He was referring to Christian love rather than romantic love. Jesus was referring to the Calvary kind of love (John 3:16) rather than physical love.

Don't be confused. Romantic love is one of the essential ingredients for a good marriage, yet at the same time it should be recognized that the home that is built on this kind of love alone has its foundation resting upon sand rather than on a solid rock.

The Bible makes it very clear that the first and greatest of the commandments requires each of us to love God with the totality of our being (Matthew 22:37). Loving our neighbor is to be our primary manner of relating to Him (v. 39).

The principle of love is interpreted to be the law by which we are to regulate our lives as children of God (James 2:8). In writing to the Ephesians, the Apostle Paul encouraged husbands to "love your wives, as Christ loved the Church and gave himself up for her, For no man ever hates his own flesh, but nourishes and cherishes it, as Christ does the Church" (Ephesians 5:25, 28-29).

When asked the question, what is love? An old man answered the question this way, "it is defined as a four-letter word consisting of two consonants (L and V), two vowels (O and E), and two fools, you and me!" (It sounds as if that man has been watching too much of Jeopardy). Another man answered the question this way, "if life is one crazy thing after another, love must be two crazy things after another." A cartoon depicts two people, a man and a woman on a dogsled in Alaska. The man feeling romantic said to the woman, "I will drive my dog team one hundred miles to say I love you," to which the woman responded, "that's a lot of mush."

Is that what love is? Two fools, you and me; two crazy things looking after each other; a lot of mush? What is love? One of the most beautiful biblical answers to that question is found in the Old Testament book, the Song of Solomon. Many of you already know that much controversy has swirled around this unique book. Some see the story to be an allegory about the love of God for His chosen people. Still others feel the story is an actual depiction of human love between a man and a woman. I am inclined to believe that it is both. The Song of Solomon is first of all a collection of love songs describing the love of a man for a woman. This human love story becomes an allegory describing God's love for His people.

The inclusion of this book in the Old Testament cannon demonstrates the sanctity of human love and the sacredness of the relationship between a man and a woman. This book provides some insights into the key ingredients of love.

The Scripture reminds us that, "Love is patient and is kind; love is not jealous or boastful; is not arrogant or rude. Love does not insist on its own way; it is not irritable or resentful; it does not rejoice at wrong, but rejoices in the right. Love bears all things, believes all things, hopes all things, endures all things. Love never ends..." (1 Corinthians 13:4-8a).

Micah, a prophet of the eighth century BC, defined mankind's duty toward God in a remarkable statement: "He has shown you O man, what is good; and what does the Lord require of you but to do justice, and to love kindness, and to walk humbly with your God?" (Micah 6:8).

It remained for Jesus to define the duty of man toward God in terms of love. "You shall love the Lord your God with all your heart, and with all your mind" (Matthew 22:37). Men sometimes find it very difficult to love God because they have not processed the ideal that God is loveable and worthy of their devotion. They have been told things about God that cause them to be frightened. God has been misrepresented. He is blamed for man's misfortune and tragedy.

We who are parents get agitated sometimes with our children or others when we have to tell them over and over again to do certain things. For example, clean up your room, don't waste that food, do your homework, go to bed, etc. Well, Jesus had the same kind of problem with his disciples. Jesus exclaimed on one occasion to them, "Do you not perceive or understand? Are your hearts hardened? (Mark 6:17). In John's Gospel (14:9), Jesus said to Phillip, "Have I been with you so long, and yet you do not know me, Phillip?" We should not be surprised that even after the Resurrection, Jesus questioned Peter concerning his love.

> When they had finished breakfast, Jesus said to Simon Peter, "Simon son of John, do you love me more than these?" He said to Him, "Yes Lord, you know that I love you." He said to him, "Feed my lambs." A second time He said to him, "Simon, son of John, do you love me?" He said to Him, "Yes, Lord; you know that I love you." He said to him, "Tend my sheep." He said to him the third time, "Simon, son of John, do you love me?" Peter was grieved because He said to him the third time, "Do you love me?" And he said to Him, "Lord, you know everything; you know that I love you." Jesus said to him, "Feed my sheep" (John 21:15-17).

Jesus wanted to be certain of Simon Peter's commitment. Much of His mission would be depending upon it. Peter, like so many of us, grew angry because of being asked the same question over and over again.

Peter's later life, as recorded in the book of Acts, shows that his yes answers carried much weight for him. Peter demonstrated his love for Jesus in deed and in action. Maybe, just maybe, he realized how important that day was in his life when he answered Jesus' same question three times with affirmation instead of denying Him three times. If Jesus asked you that same question today, how would you answer the question? What would your answer be? I pray that your answer would be the same as Peter's; Yes, Lord, You know that I love you.

Too many of us when asked to do something say yes, but in our hearts we know we have no intention of keeping our word. I read a short story a few weeks ago about a father and his young son, and this is what it said:

> Riding in the car with his father, a little boy stood up so that he could see better. "Son," said the father, "sit down in the seat," The boy sat down, but in a moment he was on his feet again. "Sit down in the seat," said the father, "and stay there." The boy sat down, but after a while he was standing. The frustrated father again told his son to, "sit down and stay in your seat!" The boy obeyed his father. However, after a moment the boy said to his father, "I'm sitting down, but in my mind I'm still standing up."[88]

If this was your son, what would you do? The Bible reminds parents to, "Train up a child in the way he should go, and when he is old he will not depart from it" (Proverbs 22:6). You may not realize it now, but if you are the father of a son, be advised, he is watching you carefully, he respects you, he studies you, and he tries to emulate you. Whether consciously or not, he wants to grow up to be just like you. He is developing life patterns: a way of thinking, a way of looking at life, evaluating it in terms of what he sees in you.

Frightening, isn't it? Diabolically frightening! Our children have big eyes and big ears. They hear and see with an acute, sharp awareness. Their minds are delicate, sensitive, like a magnetic recording tape, picking up everything. Your son is following you! Where are you leading him?

Jesus has reserved a place for you to dine with him. He wants to Feed the Lambs and Sheep. If you have not received Jesus as your Lord and Savior, do so today. Jesus is waiting for you.

Sermon Number Two

A Decision Must Be Made

The text:

When Ahab saw Elijah, Ahab said to him, "Is it you, you troubler of Israel?" And he answered, "I have not troubled Israel; but you have, and your father's house, because you have forsaken the commandments of the Lord and followed the Baals. Now therefore send and gather all Israel to me at Mount Carmel, and the four hundred and fifty

prophets of Baal and the four hundred prophets of Asherah who eat at Jezebel's table."
— 1 Kings 18:17-19

A Decision Must Be Made

According to Hebrews Chapter 11 and verse 1, "Now faith is the answer of the things hoped for, the conviction of things not seen." The Bible explains further, "And without faith it is impossible to please Him. For whoever would draw near to God must believe that He exists and that He rewards those who seek Him" (Hebrews 11:6).

It is not the big decisions, the complicated, elaborate ones that determine a man's or a woman's destiny. It is the every day simple choices that set the stage, tune a man's will, pre-determine what big decisions will be when things are not going his way. Generally speaking, big decisions are few and far between, how a brother reacts, what he does with the big issue is already decided on the basis of the many little choices he makes from day to day. Little choices determine habits. Habits carve and mold character. Character makes the big decisions!

God calls all people to a place of decision where they must abandon their personal ideals and variant beliefs to embrace the only true Gospel of salvation. Such a poignant message always engenders some conflicts.

Too many of our brothers and sisters hear the Word of God, the Good News and do nothing. At no time does there seem to be any great issues involved. They get used to hearing and doing absolutely nothing! It becomes easier and easier to hear without hearing, to see without seeing, to move and not to decide, until at last nothing bothers them. They do not hear, they do not see, nor can they be moved!

In our text today (1 Kings 18:17ff), King Ahab asked Elijah the anointed prophet this question, "Is it you, you troubler of Israel?" Things haven't changed, there are people just like Ahab. They will ask you a question and before you can answer the question they will give you an answer. But the Bible tells us that Elijah did answer the question and set the record straight. "I have not troubled Israel; but you have and your father's house, because you have forsaken the commandments of the Lord and followed the Baals" (1 Kings 18:18). Baal was the god of the Phoenicia and Canaanitish Tribes. Balaam means many gods.

Let me tell you something about the evil King Ahab. Ahab was the son of Omri and the seventh King of Israel (848-850 BC). Ahab was efficient and strong in manipulative and administrative powers, but weak and vacillating in the face of his powerful wife, Jezebel. Jezebel was a clever and determined woman, devoted to the worship of Baal and Asherah and determined to substitute their worship for that of the true God.

Elijah on the other hand was a great prophet. Virtually nothing is known of his background and parentage. In his first recorded act, he appeared before King Ahab and predicted a severe drought. Now Ahab and Elijah meet at Mount Carmel with the prophets of Baal. Elijah stands tall and say with authority probably pointing his bony finger and saying to Ahab and the prophets, "How long will you go limping with two different opinions? If the Lord is God, follow him; but if Baal then follow Him. And the people did not answer him a word" (1 Kings 18:22).

So, Elijah by this time is feeling pretty good and boldly says, "I, even I only, am left a prophet of the Lord; but Baal's prophets are four hundred and fifty men. Let two bulls be given to us; and let them choose one for themselves, and cut it in pieces and lay it on the wood, but put no fire to it; and I will prepare the other bull and lay it on the wood, and put no fire to it. And you can call on the name of your god and I will call on the name of the Lord; and the God who answers by fire, he is God." "And all the people answered it is well spoken." Then Elijah said to the prophets of Baal, "Choose for yourselves one bull and prepare it first, for you are many; and call on the name of your god, but put no fire to it" (1 Kings 18:23).

The four hundred and fifty prophets of Baal took the bull which was given them, and they prepared it, and called on the name of Baal from morning until noon, saying, O, Baal answer us! But there was no voice, and no answer.

Picture in your mind four hundred and fifty prophets limping around the altar getting no answer from their god, Baal. So at noon Elijah mocked them, saying, "Cry aloud for he is a god; either he is musing, or he has gone aside, or he is on a journey, or perhaps he is asleep and must be awakened" (1 Kings 18:27).

The Bible tells us that, "the prophets were so frustrated that they cried aloud, and cut themselves after their custom with swords and lances, until the blood gushed out upon them" (1 Kings 18:28). And as midday passed, they raved on until the time of the offering of the oblation, (which was about 3 P.M.) but there was no voice; no one answered, no one heeded.

The Bible goes on to say, "Then Elijah said to all the people, 'Come near to me;' and all the people came near to him. Elijah the prophet of God repaired the altar that had been thrown down. Then Elijah took twelve stones, according to the number of the tribes of the sons of Jacob, to whom the word of the Lord came, saying, 'Israel shall be your name;' and with the stones he built the altar in the name of the Lord" (1 Kings 18:30-31).

Elijah made a trench around the altar, as great as would contain two measures of seed. And he put the wood in order, and cut the bull in pieces and laid it on the wood. And he said, "Fill four jars with water, and pour it on the burnt offering, and on the wood. This Elijah did three times. There was so much water around the altar that it filled the trench around it" (1 Kings 18:32-34).

At the time of the offering of the oblation, Elijah the prophet came near and prayed, saying, "O Lord, God of Abraham, Isaac, and Israel, let it be known this day that I am thy servant, and that I have done all these things at thy word. Answer me, O Lord, answer me, that this people may know that thou, O Lord, art God, and that thou has turned their hearts back" (1 Kings 18:35-36).

Then the fire of the Lord fell, and consumed the burnt offering, and the wood, and the stones, and the dust, and licked up the water that was in the trench.

When the people saw what had taken place, they fell on their faces; and they said, "The Lord, He is God; the Lord, He is God" (1 Kings 18:39).

Elijah said to God's people, "seize the prophets of Baal; let not one of them escape" (1 Kings 18:40). The people did as Elijah commanded them, and brought the prophets of Baal down to the brook Kishon, and killed them there.

We find in Psalm 51 the story of King David when Nathan the prophet came unto him after he had gone into Bathsheba. David realized his sins and looked to God saying, "Have mercy on me, O God, according to thy steadfast love; according to thy abundant mercy blot out my transgressions. Wash me thoroughly from my iniquity, and cleanse me from my sins!" "...Create in me a clean heart, O God, and put a new and right spirit within me. Restore to me the joy of thy salvation and uphold me with a willing spirit" (Psalm 51:1-2; 10-12).

In Acts, the 25th and 26th Chapters, the Apostle Paul has been arrested for preaching Jesus. Paul had been in jail for two or more years when he is brought before King Agrippa. The Apostle Paul tells the King about his conversion. After pleading with Agrippa to become a Christian, Paul is noticing the King's body language and it is saying something like this. I don't know if I am ready for this! I have heard about all the great things that Jesus and his disciples have done. I can't make up my mind. Can't you see I am a King already!

Paul perceived in his spirit that he is not getting through to King Agrippa, so he said to him, ". . . I know that you believe." And Agrippa said to Paul, "In a short time you think to make me a Christian!" (Acts 26:27-28).

How about you? Don't be like King Agrippa! This is your day. Jesus is saying to us, "Behold, I stand at the door and knock; if any one hears my voice and opens the door, I will come in and eat with him, and he with me."

I read a story recently about two friends entitled, Sand and Stone that goes like this:

> A story tells that two friends were walking through the desert. During some point of the journey, they had an argument, and one friend slapped the other one in the face. The one who

got slapped was hurt, but without saying anything, he wrote in the sand. Today my best friend slapped me in the face.

They kept on walking, until they found an oasis where they decided to take a bath. The one who had been slapped got stuck in the mire and started drowning, but his friend saved him. After he recovered from the near drowning, he wrote on a stone.

Today my best friend saved my life. The friend, who slapped and saved his best friend asked him, "After I hurt you, you wrote in the sand, and now, you write on a stone, why?"

The other friend replied, "when someone hurts us, we should write it down in sand, where the winds of forgiveness can erase it away, but when someone does something good for us, we must engrave it in stone where no one can ever erase it." Learn to write your hurts in the sand and to carve your blessings on a stone.[89]

I know that you have heard the message! Now, it's your time to decide. If you haven't made a decision to follow Jesus, this is your day of deliverance.

The Conclusion

Jesus said to them again, "Peace be with you. As the Father has sent me, even so I send you."
— John 20:21

Throughout this book it has been my purpose to relate to you the importance of *Looking for God's People in Rural Places*. The rural church is best prepared to equip its members and community when they are properly nourished and cared for by the rural minister.

In order to be the united force God wants the rural church and community to be, they need to accept their limitations and the complementary relationship God intends them to have with one another.

Every dimension of the rural church and community has a particular calling. Fulfilling these callings creates a cycle of independent activities and mutual blessings. The rural minister teaches the congregation how to go out to look for God's people and bring them to the Church for fellowship. The new converts, in turn, go out to evangelize resulting in new church life, and the cycle continues.

In the rural community some hear the Gospel many times. However, some hear it once. Sadly, some never hear it at all! Our response to hearing the Gospel is important, for it is God's method of calling sinners to repentance. When a man, woman, boy, or girl does not accept the Gospel, they are rejecting it and, therefore, without excuse.

The rural church must not see the Great Commission as an addendum to the Church program. It must be the Church program. It is not an optional extra but the driving force and central vision for the rural minister and the congregation.

Mission is then a matter of calling, and taking time to test that calling. If persons are called into missionary service, it is only reasonable to expect them to be active in the Church evangelistic activities. The rural church should joyfully embrace the task of *Looking for God's People in Rural Places* and make saints out of them.

May we always respond to the Gospel of Jesus Christ with acceptance and faith and receive that which the Lord has prepared for us. The future of the rural church and community is in God's hand. He will judge its success or failure.

Endnotes

[1] James D. Smart, *The Rebirth of Ministry* (Philadelphia: The Westminster Press, 1974), p. 37.

[2] Wallace C. Smith, *The Church in the Life of the Family* (Valley Forge, PA: Judson Press, 1971), p. 108.

[3] Royce A. Rose, *Professional Competencies Needed by Pastors of Small Rural Churches as Perceived by Pastors, Lay Leaders, and Denomination Church Developers.* Unpublished doctoral dissertation (Ed.D.) Southern Baptist Theological Seminary, 1983.

[4] William Smith, *A Dictionary of the Bible* (Nashville: Thomas Nelson Publishers, 1962), p. 117.

[5] Phillip Keller, *A Shepherd Looks At Psalm 23* (Grand Rapids, MI: Zondervan Publishing House, 1970), pp. 15-17.

[6] Friedrich Hegel, *On Christianity: Early Theological Writings* (Chicago: Harper Torchbooks, 1948), pp. 280-301.

[7] Alan Richardson and John Bowden, *The Westminster Dictionary of Christian Theology* (Philadelphia: The Westminster Press, 1983), pp. 496-498.

[8] Henrietta C. Mears, *What the Bible is All About* (Minneapolis, MN: Gospel Light Publications, 1966), p. 1.

[9] John F. Wilson, *Religion: A Preface* (Englewood Cliffs, NJ: Prentice-Hall, 1982), p. 170.

[10] Richard J. Coleman, *Issues of Theological Conflict* (Grand Rapids, MI: William B. Eerdmans Publishing Company, 1980), p. 7.

[11] *Encyclopedia Americana* International Ed. Volume 26 (New York: Americana Corporation. 1965), p. 516.

[12] *Ibid.*, p. 517.

[13] A. W. Tozer, *Man: The Dwelling Place of God* (Harrisburg, PA: Christian Publication, 1966), p. 85.

[14] William Steuart McBirnie, *The Search for the Twelve Apostles* (Wheaton, IL: Tyndale House Publishers, 1977), p. 16.

[15] Findley B. Edge, *The Greening of the Church* (Waco, TX: World Books Publishers, 1971), p. 109.

[16] Monroe R. Saunders, Sr., *The Book of Church Order and Discipline of the United Church Of Jesus Christ (Apostolic)*, (Washington, DC, 1965), p. 22.

[17] John F. Wilson, *Religion: A Preface* (Englewood Cliffs, NJ: Prentice-Hall. 1982), p. 97.

[18] Thomas H. Groome, *Christian Religious Education: Sharing Our Story and Vision* (San Francisco: Harper & Row, 1980), p. 48.

[19] Ezra Earl Jones, *Strategies for New Churches* (New York: Harper & Row Publishers, 1972), pp. 28-29.

[20] Lyle E. Schaller, *The Small Church is Different!* (Nashville: Abingdon Press, 1982), pp. 28-29.

[21] Wilson, *Religion: A Preface*, p. 46.

[22] Lyle E. Schaller, *The First Parish* (Philadelphia: The Westminster Press, 1983), p. 28.

[23] Gerald J. Jud, Edgar W. Mills, Jr. and Genevieve Walters Burch, *Ex-Pastors: Why Men Leave the Parish Ministry* (Boston: Pilgrim Press, 1975), p. 49.

[24] Shirley E. Greene, *Ferment on the Fringe; Studies of Rural Churches in Transition* (Philadelphia: Christian Education Press, 1960), p. 3.

[25] Richard Stoll Armstrong, *The Pastor As Evangelist* (Philadelphia: The Westminster Press, 1984), p. 20.

[26] *Ibid.*, p. 41.

[27] Rockwell C. Smith, *Rural Ministry and the Changing Community* (Nashville: Abingdon Press, 1991), p. 13.

[28] Wayne Pounders, *Commitment to Evangelism* (Hazelwood, MO: Pentecostal Publishing House, 1994), p 28-29.

[29] Gaines S. Dobbins, *A Ministering Church* (Nashville: Broadman Press, 1960), pp. 195-196.

[30] J. D. Douglas, Walter A. Elwell, and Peter Toon. *The Concise Dictionary of the Christian Tradition: Doctrine, Liturgy, History* (Grand Rapids, MI: 1989), p. 146.

[31] Keith Cook, *The First Parish: A Pastor's Survival Manual* (Philadelphia: The Westminster Press, 1993), p. 103

[32] *Ibid.*, p. 103

[33] *Ibid.*, p. 104.

[34] Richard Stoll Armstrong, *The Pastor As Evangelist* (Philadelphia: The Westminster Press, 1984), p. 33-34.

[35] Gordon Clinard, *Evangelism: The Cutting Edge*. (Atlanta: Home Mission Board, 1973), p. 34.

[36] J. D. Douglas, *The Calling of An Evangelist: The Second International Congress for Itinerant Evangelists* (Minneapolis, MN: World Wide Publication, 1987), p. 131.

[37] *Ibid.*, p. 141.

[38] Angela Erenia, *Rural Roots* (Washington, DC: Rural Ministry Institute, 1986), p. 3.

[39] Lyle E. Schaller, *The Small Church is Different!* (Nashville: Abingdon Press, 1982), pp. 28-29.

[40] H. Wayne House, *The High Calling to Servanthood* (Cleveland: Union Gospel Press, 1988), p. 3.

[41] *Ibid.*, p. 3.

[42] G. Willis Bennett, *Effective Urban Church Ministry* (Nashville: Broadman Press, 1983), p. 49.

[43] William H. Willimon & Robert L. Wilson, *Preaching and Worship in the Small Church* (Nashville: Abingdon Press, 1982), p. 36.

[44] Barbara Brown Zikmund, *Discovering the Church*. (Philadelphia: The Westminster Press, 1983), p. 15.

[45] Edward A. Rauff, *Why People Join the Church: An Exploratory Study* (Nashville: Pilgrim Press, 1972), p. 89.

[46] Alan Richardson and John Bowden, *The Westminster Dictionary of Christian Theology* (Philadelphia: The Westminster Press, 1983), pp. 316-318.

[47] Richard M. Davis, *The Neighborhood Network* (Hazelwood, MO: Pentecostal Publishing House, 1999), p. 46.

[48] William Henry Jones, *Communicating the Gospel of Jesus Christ in America's Rural Church and Community*. Unpublished doctoral dissertation (D.Min.) Howard University School of Divinity, 1988.

[49] Gaines S. Dobbins, *A Ministering Church* (Nashville: Broadman Press, 1960), p. 165.

[50] Trent C. Butler, ed. *Holman Bible Dictionary* (Nashville: Holman Bible Publishers, 1991), p. 306.

[51] H. H. London, *Principles and Techniques of Vocational Guidance* (Philadelphia: The Westminster Press, 1974), p. 9.

[52] Raymond Hostie, *Pastoral Counseling*. Translated by Gilbert Barth. (New York: Sheed and Ward, Inc. 1966), p. 50.

[53] Wayne E. Oates, *Pastoral Counseling* (Philadelphia: The Westminster Press, 1974), p. 9.

[54] *Ibid.*, p. 9.

[55] Marvin G. Gilbert and Raymond T. Brock, eds. *The Holy Spirit & Counseling* (Peabody, MA: Hendrickson Publishers, 1985), p. 123.

[56] Oates, *op. cit.*, p. 142.

[57] *Ibid.*, p. 142.

[58] Eugene C. Kennedy, *Crisis Counseling: An Essential Guide for Nonprofessional Counselors* (New York: The Continuum Publishing Co., 1986), p. 17.

[59] J. Randall Nichols, *The Restoring Word: Preaching As Pastoral Communication* (San Francisco: Harper & Row Publishers, 1987), p. 67.

[60] Gene A. Getz, *Sharpening the Focus of the Church* (Chicago: Moody Press, 1974), p. 107.

[61] Edgar N. Jackson, *Parish Counseling* (New York: Jason Aronson, Inc., 1983), p. 41.

[62] J. Keith Cook, *The First Parish: A Pastor's Survival Manual* (Philadelphia: The Westminster Press, 1985), p. 105.

[63] James E. Carter, *The Mission of the Church* (Nashville: Broadman Press, 1974), p. 11.

[64] William Barclay, *The All-Sufficient Christ; Studies in Paul's Letter to the Colossians* (London, England: SCM Press, 1963), pp. 111-112.

[65] Carter, p. 12.

[66] W. L. Howse and W. O. Thomas, *A Dynamic Church: Spirit and Structure for the Seventies* (Nashville: Convention Press, 1969), p. 70.

[67] Paul O. Madsen, *The Small Church – Valid, Vital, Victorious* (Valley Forge, PA: Judson Press, 1975), p. 64.

[68] Richard Stoll Armstrong, *The Pastor-Evangelist in Worship* (Philadelphia: The Westminster Press, 1986), p. 41.

[69] Hendrikus Berkhof, *Christian Faith: An Introduction to the Study of the Faith* Translated by Sierd Woudstra. (Grand Rapids, MI: William B. Eerdmans Publishing Company, 1979), p. 16.

[70] Alan Richardson and John Bowden, *The Westminster Dictionary of Christian Theology* (Philadelphia: The Westminster Press, 1983), p. 207.

[71] Richard M. Davis, *The Book of Hebrews: Faith Possibilities* (Hazelwood, MO: Pentecostal Publishing House. 2002), p. 77.

[72] Richard C. Halverson, *No Greater Power: Perspectives for Days of Pleasure* (Portland, OR : Multnomah Press, 1986), p. 195.

[73] James W. Cox, ed. *The Minister's Manual* (San Francisco: Harper Collins Publishers, 1987), p. 303.

[74] Paul Little, *How to Give Away Your Faith: With Study Questions for Individuals or Groups* (Downers Grove, IL: InterVarsity Press, 1988), p. 30.

[75] *Ibid.*, p. 30.

[76] Davis, *The Book of Hebrews*. p. 77.

[77] *Ibid.*, p. 78.

[78] Norman Vincent Peale and Smiley Blanton. *Faith is the Answer; A Pastor and a Psychiatrist Discuss Your Problems* (Pawling, NY: Foundation for Christian Living, 1955), p. 13.

[79] H. L. R. Deck, "I Take Thy Promise, Lord." *Hymns*, ed. Paul Beckwith (Chicago: InterVarsity Press, 1947), p. 6.

[80] Alan Richardson and John Bowden, *The Westminster Dictionary of Christian Theology* (Philadelphia: The Westminster Press, 1983), p. 459.

[81] *Ibid.*, p. 459.

[82] Myron R. Chartier, *Preaching As Communication: An Interpersonal Perspective* (Nashville: The Parthenon Press, 1981), p. 21.

[83] Charles Simeon, *Evangelical Preaching* (Portland, OR: Multnomah Press, 1986), p. xix.

[84] Hugh Evan Hopkins, *Charles Simeon Extraordinary* (Bramcote, England: Grove Books, 1979), pp. 291-410.

[85] William C. Martin, *The Layman's Bible Encyclopedia* (Nashville: The Southwestern Company, 1964), p. 644.

[86] Richard M. Davis, *The Message of Acts* (Hazelwood, MO: Pentecostal House 2003), p. 91.

[87] F. Dean Lueking, *Preaching: The Art of Connecting God and People* (Waco, TX: Word Books Publishers, 1985), p. 23.

[88] Richard M. Davis, *Prophecy to Be Fulfilled* (Hazelwood, MO: Pentecostal Publishing House, 1999), p. 60.

[89] This story was published in the *South Hill Enterprise*, December 10, 2003. Author unknown. p. 8.

[90] James D. Smart, *The Rebirth of Ministry* (Philadelphia: The Westminster Press, 1974), p. 37.

[91] Wallace C. Smith, *The Church in the Life of the Family* (Valley Forge, PA: Judson Press, 1971), p. 108.

[92] Royce A. Rose, *Professional Competencies Needed by Pastors of Small Rural Churches as Perceived by Pastors, Lay Leaders, and Denomination Church Developers.* Unpublished

doctoral dissertation (Ed.D.) Southern Baptist Theological Seminary, 1983.

[93] William Smith, *A Dictionary of the Bible* (Nashville: Thomas Nelson Publishers, 1962). p. 117.

[94] Phillip Keller, *A Shepherd Looks At Psalm 23* (Grand Rapids, MI: Zondervan Publishing House, 1970), pp. 15-7.

[95] Friedrich Hegel, *On Christianity: Early Theological Writings* (Chicago: Harper Torchbooks, 1948), pp. 280-301.

[96] Alan Richardson and John Bowden, *The Westminster Dictionary of Christian Theology* (Philadelphia: The Westminster Press, 1983), pp. 496-498.

[97] Henrietta C. Mears, *What the Bible is All About* (Minneapolis, MN: Gospel Light Publications, 1966), p. 1.

[98] John F. Wilson, *Religion: A Preface* (Englewood Cliffs, NJ: Prentice-Hall, 1982), p. 170.

[99] Richard J. Coleman, *Issues of Theological Conflict* (Grand Rapids, MI: William B. Eerdmans Publishing Company, 1980), p. 7.

[100] *Encyclopedia Americana* International Ed. Volume 26 (New York: Americana Corporation, 1965), p. 516.

[101] *Ibid.*, p. 517.

[102] A. W. Tozer, *Man: The Dwelling Place of God* (Harrisburg, PA: Christian Publication, 1966), p. 85.

[103] William Steuart McBirnie, *The Search for the Twelve Apostles* (Wheaton, IL: Tyndale House Publishers, 1977), p. 16.

[104] Findley B. Edge, *The Greening of the Church*. (Waco, TX: World Books Publishers, 1971), p. 109.

[105] Monroe R. Saunders, Sr., *The Book of Church Order and Discipline of the United Church Of Jesus Christ (Apostolic)*, (Washington, DC, 1965), p. 22.

[106] John F. Wilson, *Religion: A Preface* (Englewood Cliffs, NJ: Prentice-Hall. 1982), p. 97.

[107] Thomas H. Groome, *Christian Religious Education: Sharing Our Story and Vision* (San Francisco: Harper & Row, 1980), p. 48.

[108] Ezra Earl Jones, *Strategies for New Churches* (New York: Harper & Row Publishers, 1972), pp. 28-29.

[109] Lyle E. Schaller, *The Small Church is Different!* (Nashville: Abingdon Press, 1982), pp. 28-29.

[110] Wilson, *Religion: A Preface*, p. 46.

[111] Lyle E. Schaller, *The First Parish* (Philadelphia: The Westminster Press, 1983), p. 28.

[112] Gerald J. Jud, Edgar W. Mills, Jr. and Genevieve Walters Burch, *Ex-Pastors: Why Men Leave the Parish Ministry* (Boston: Pilgrim Press, 1975), p. 49.

[113] Shirley E. Greene, *Ferment on the Fringe; Studies of Rural Churches in Transition.*(Philadelphia: Christian Education Press, 1960), p. 3.

[114] Richard Stoll Armstrong, *The Pastor As Evangelist* (Philadelphia: The Westminster Press, 1984), p. 20.

[115] *Ibid.*, p. 41.

[116] Rockwell C. Smith, *Rural Ministry and the Changing Community* (Nashville: Abingdon Press, 1991), p. 13.

[117] Wayne Pounders, *Commitment to Evangelism* (Hazelwood, MO: Pentecostal Publishing House, 1994), p. 28-29.

[118] Gaines S. Dobbins, *A Ministering Church* (Nashville: Broadman Press, 1960), pp. 195-196.

[119] J. D. Douglas, Walter A. Elwell, and Peter Toon, *The Concise Dictionary of the Christian Tradition: Doctrine, Liturgy, History* (Grand Rapids, MI: Zondervan Publishing House, 1989), p. 146.

[120] Keith Cook, *The First Parish: A Pastor's Survival Manual* (Philadelphia: The Westminster Press, 1993), p. 103

[121] *Ibid.*, p. 103

[122] *Ibid.*, p. 104.

[123] Richard Stoll Armstrong, *The Pastor As Evangelist* (Philadelphia: The Westminster Press, 1984), p. 33-34.

[124] Gordon Clinard, *Evangelism: The Cutting Edge* (Atlanta: Home Mission Board, 1973), p. 34.

[125] J. D. Douglas, *The Calling of An Evangelist: The Second International Congress for Itinerant Evangelists* (Minneapolis, MN: World Wide Publication, 1987), p. 131.

[126] *Ibid.*, p. 141.

[127] Angela Erenia, *Rural Roots* (Washington, DC: Rural Ministry Institute, 1986), p. 3.

[128] Lyle E. Schaller, *The Small Church is Different!* (Nashville: Abingdon Press, 1982), pp. 28-29.

[129] H. Wayne House, *The High Calling to Servanthood* (Cleveland: Union Gospel Press, 1988), p. 3.

[130] *Ibid.*, p. 3.

[131] G. Willis Bennett, *Effective Urban Church Ministry* (Nashville: Broadman Press, 1983), p. 49.

[132] William H. Willimon & Robert L. Wilson, *Preaching and Worship in the Small Church* (Nashville: Abingdon Press, 1982), p. 36.

[133] Barbara Brown Zikmund, *Discovering the Church* (Philadelphia: The Westminster Press, 1983), p. 15.

[134] Edward A. Rauff, *Why People Join the Church: An Exploratory Study* (Nashville: Pilgrim Press, 1972), p. 89.

[135] Alan Richardson and John Bowden, *The Westminster Dictionary of Christian Theology* (Philadelphia: The Westminster Press, 1983), pp. 316-318.

[136] Richard M. Davis, *The Neighborhood Network* (Hazelwood, MO: Pentecostal Publishing House, 1999), p. 46.

[137] William Henry Jones, *Communicating the Gospel of Jesus Christ in America's Rural Church and Community*. Unpublished doctoral dissertation (D.Min.) Howard University School of Divinity, 1988.

[138] Gaines S. Dobbins, *A Ministering Church* (Nashville: Broadman Press, 1960), p. 165.

[139] Trent C. Butler, ed. *Holman Bible Dictionary* (Nashville: Holman Bible Publishers, 1991), p. 306.

[140] H. H. London, *Principles and Techniques of Vocational Guidance* (Philadelphia: The Westminster Press, 1974), p. 9.

[141] Raymond Hostie, *Pastoral Counseling*. Translated by Gilbert Barth (New York: Sheed and Ward, Inc. 1966), p. 50.

[142] Wayne E. Oates, *Pastoral Counseling* (Philadelphia: The Westminster Press, 1974), p. 9.

[143] *Ibid.*, p. 9.

[144] Marvin G. Gilbert and Raymond T. Brock, eds. *The Holy Spirit & Counseling* (Peabody, MA: Hendrickson Publishers, 1985), p. 123.

[145] Oates, *op. cit.*, p. 142.

[146] *Ibid.*, p. 142.

[147] Eugene C. Kennedy, *Crisis Counseling: An Essential Guide for Nonprofessional Counselors* (New York: The Continuum Publishing Co., 1986), p. 17.

[148] J. Randall Nichols, *The Restoring Word: Preaching As Pastoral Communication* (San Francisco: Harper & Row Publishers, 1987), p. 67.

[149] Gene A. Getz, *Sharpening the Focus of the Church* (Chicago: Moody Press, 1974), p. 107.

[150] Edgar N. Jackson, *Parish Counseling* (New York: Jason Aronson, Inc., 1983), p. 41.

[151] J. Keith Cook, *The First Parish: A Pastor's Survival Manual* (Philadelphia: The Westminster Press, 1985), p. 105.

[152] James E. Carter, *The Mission of the Church* (Nashville: Broadman Press, 1974), p. 11.

[153] William Barclay, *The All-Sufficient Christ; Studies in Paul's Letter to the Colossians* (London, England: SCM Press, 1963), pp. 111-112.

[154] Carter, p. 12.

[155] W. L. Howse and W. O. Thomas, *A Dynamic Church: Spirit and Structure for the Seventies* (Nashville: Convention Press, 1969), p. 70.

[156] Paul O. Madsen, *The Small Church – Valid, Vital, Victorious* (Valley Forge, PA: Judson Press, 1975), p. 64.

[157] Richard Stoll Armstrong, *The Pastor-Evangelist in Worship* (Philadelphia: The Westminster Press, 1986), p. 41.

[158] Hendrikus Berkhof, *Christian Faith: An Introduction to the Study of the Faith*. Translated by Sierd Woudstra. (Grand Rapids, MI: William B. Eerdmans Publishing Company, 1979), p. 16.

[159] Alan Richardson and John Bowden, *The Westminster Dictionary of Christian Theology* (Philadelphia: The Westminster Press, 1983), p. 207.

[160] Richard M. Davis, *The Book of Hebrews: Faith Possibilities* (Hazelwood, MO: Pentecostal Publishing House, 2002), p. 77.

[161] Richard C. Halverson, *No Greater Power: Perspective for Days of Pleasure* (Portland, OR : Multnomah Press, 1986), p. 195.

[162] James W. Cox, ed. *The Minister's Manual* (San Francisco: Harper Collins Publishers, 1987), p. 303.

[163] Paul Little, *How to Give Away Your Faith: With Study Questions for Individuals or Groups* (Downers Grove, IL: InterVarsity Press, 1988), p. 30.

[164] *Ibid.*, p. 30.

[165] Davis, *The Book of Hebrews*. p. 77.

[166] *Ibid.*, p. 78.

[167] *Ibid.*, p. 78

[168] Norman Vincent Peale and Smiley Blanton. *Faith is the Answer; A Pastor and a Psychiatrist Discuss Your Problems* (Pawling, NY: Foundation for Christian Living, 1955), p. 13.

[169] H. L. R. Deck, "I Take Thy Promise, Lord." *Hymns*, ed. Paul Beckwith (Chicago: InterVarsity Press, 1947), p. 6.

[170] Alan Richardson and John Bowden, *The Westminster Dictionary of Christian Theology* (Philadelphia: The Westminster Press, 1983), p. 459.

[171] *Ibid.*, p. 459.

[172] Myron R. Chartier, *Preaching As Communication: An Interpersonal Perspective* (Nashville: The Parthenon Press, 1981), p. 21.

[173] Charles Simeon, *Evangelical Preaching* (Portland, OR: Multnomah Press, 1986), p. 6.

[174] Hugh Evan Hopkins, *Charles Simeon Extraordinary* (Bramcote, England: Grove Books, 1979), pp. 291-410.

[175] William C. Martin, *The Layman's Bible Encyclopedia* (Nashville: The Southwestern Company, 1964), p. 644.

[176] Richard M. Davis, *The Message of Acts* (Hazelwood, MO: Pentecostal House 2003), p. 91.

[177] F. Dean Lueking, *Preaching: The Art of Connecting God and People* (Waco, TX: Word Books Publishers, 1985), p. 23.

[178] Richard M. Davis, *Prophecy to Be Fulfilled.* (Hazelwood, MO: Pentecostal Publishing House, 1999), p. 60.

[179] This story was published in the *South Hill Enterprise*, December 10, 2003. Author unknown. p. 8.

Selected Bibliography

Armstrong, Richard Stoll. *The Pastor As Evangelist.* Philadelphia: The Westminster Press, 1984.

———. *The Pastor-Evangelist in Worship.* Philadelphia: The Westminster Press, 1986.

Barclay, William. *The All-Sufficient Christ; Studies in Paul's Letter to the Colossians.* London, England: SCM Press, 1963.

Bennett, G. Willis. *Effective Urban Church Ministry.* Nashville: Broadman Press, 1983.

Berkhof, Hendrikus. *Christian Faith: An Introduction to the Study of the Faith.* Translated by Sierd Woudstra. Grand Rapids, MI: William B. Eerdmans Publishing Company, 1979.

Butler, Trent C. ed. *Holman Bible Dictionary.* Nashville: Holman Bible Publishers, 1991.

Carter, James E. *The Mission of the Church.* Nashville: Broadman Press, 1974.

Chartier, Myron Raymond. *Preaching As Communication: An Interpersonal Perspective.* Nashville: The Parthenon Press, 1981.

Clinard, Gordon. *Evangelism: The Cutting Edge.* Atlanta: Home Mission Board, 1973.

Cox, James W., ed. *The Minster's Manual.* San Francisco: Harper Collins Publishers, 1987.

Cook, J. Keith. *The First Parish: A Pastor's Survival Manual.* Philadelphia: The Westminster Press, 1983.

Davis, Richard M. *The Neighborhood Network.* Hazelwood, MO: Pentecostal Publishing House, 1999.

———. *The Book of Hebrews: Faith Possibilities.* Hazelwood, MO: Pentecostal Publishing House, 2002.

———. *The Message of Acts 1-14*. Hazelwood, MO: Pentecostal House, 2003.

———. *Prophecy to Be Fulfilled*. Hazelwood, MO: Pentecostal Publishing House, 1999.

Deck, H. L. R. *"I Take Thy Promise, Lord" Hymns*. Ed. Paul Beckwith. Downers Grove, IL: InterVarsity Press, 1947.

Dobbins, Gains S. *A Ministering Church*. Nashville: Broadman Press, 1960.

Douglas, J. D., ed. *The Calling of An Evangelist: The Second International Congress for Itinerant Evangelists*. Minneapolis, MN: Word Wide Publications, 1987.

Douglas, J. D., Walter A. Elwell, and Peter Toon. *The Concise Dictionary of the Christian Tradition: Doctrine, Liturgy, History*. Grand Rapids, MI: Zondervan Publishing House, 1989.

Edge, Findley B. *The Greening of the Church*. Waco, TX: Word Books Publishers, 1971.

Erenia, Angela. *Rural Roots*. Washington, DC: Rural Ministry Institute, 1986.

Getz, Gene A. *Sharpening the Focus of the Church*. Chicago: Moody Press, 1974.

Gilbert, Marvin G. and Raymond T. Brock, eds. *The Holy Spirit & Counseling*. Peabody, MA: Hendrickson Publishers, 1985.

Greene, Shirley E. *Ferment on the Fringe: Studies of Rural Churches in Transition*. Philadelphia: Christian Education Press, 1960.

Groome, Thomas H. *Christian Religious Education: Sharing Our Story and Vision*. San Francisco: Harper & Row, 1980.

Halverson, Richard C. *No Greater Power: Perspective for Days of Pleasure*. Portland, OR: Multnomah Press, 1986.

Hegel, Friedrich. Translated by T. M. Knox. *On Christianity: Early Theological Writings*. Chicago: Harper Torchbooks, 1948.

Hopkins, Hugh Evan. *Charles Simeon Extraordinary*. Bramcote, England: Grove Books, 1979.

Hostie, Raymond. *Pastoral Counseling*. Translated by Gilbert Barth. New York: Sheed and Ward, Inc., 1966.

House, H. Wayne. *The High Calling to Servanthood.* Cleveland, OH: Union Gospel Press, 1988.

Howse, W. L. and Thomas, W. O. *A Dynamic Church: Spirit and Structure for the Seventies.* Nashville: Convention Press, 1969.

Jackson, Edgar N. *Parish Counseling.* New York: Jason Aronson, Inc., 1983.

Jones, Ezra Earl. *Strategies for New Churches.* New York: Harper & Row Publishers, 1972.

Jones, William H. *Communicating the Gospel of Jesus Christ in America's Rural Church and Community.* Unpublished doctoral dissertation (D.Min.), Howard University School of Divinity, 1988.

Jud, Gerald J., Edgar W. Mills, Jr., and Genevieve Walters Burch. *Ex-Pastors: Why Men Leave the Parish Ministry.* Boston: Pilgrim Press, 1975.

Keller, W. Phillip. *A Shepherd Looks At Psalm 23.* Grand Rapids, MI: Zondervan Publishing House, 1970.

Kennedy, Eugene C. *Crisis Counseling: An Essential Guide for Nonprofessional Counselors.* New York: The Continuum Publishing Company, 1986.

Little, Paul. *How to Give Away Your Faith: With Study Questions for Individuals or Groups.* Downers Grove, IL: InterVarsity Press, 1988.

London, H. H. *Principles and Techniques of Vocational Guidance.* Philadelphia: The Westminster Press, 1994.

Lueking, F. Dean. *Preaching: The Art of Connecting God and People.* Waco, TX: Word Books Publishers, 1985.

Madsen, Paul O. *The Small Church – Valid, Vital, Victorious.* Valley Forge, PA: Judson Press, 1975.

Martin, William C. *The Layman's Bible Encyclopedia.* Nashville: The Southwestern Company, 1964.

McBirnie, William Steuart. *The Search for the Twelve Apostles.* Wheaton, IL: Tyndale House Publishers, 1977.

Mears, Henrietta C. *What the Bible is All About.* Minneapolis, MN: Gospel Light Publications, 1966.

Nichols, J. Randall. *The Restoring Word: Preaching As Pastoral Communication.* San Francisco: Harper & Row Publishers, 1987.

Oates, Wayne E. *Pastoral Counseling*. Philadelphia: The Westminster Press, 1974.

Peale, Norman Vincent and Smiley Blanton. *Faith is the Answer: A Pastor and a Psychiatrist Discuss Your Problems*. Pawling, NY: Foundation for Christian Living, 1955.

Pounders, Wayne. *Commitments to Evangelism*. Hazelwood, MO: Pentecostal Publishing House, 1994.

Rauff, Edward A. *Why People Join the Church: An Exploratory Study*. Nashville: Pilgrim Press, 1972.

Richardson, Alan and John Bowden. *The Westminster Dictionary of Christian Theology*. Philadelphia: The Westminster Press, 1983.

Rose, Royce A. *Professional Competencies Needed by Pastors of Small Rural Churches as Perceived by Pastors, Lay Leaders, and Denomination Church Developers*. Unpublished doctoral dissertation (Ed.D.) Southern Baptist Theological Seminary, 1983.

Saunders, Sr., Monroe R. *The Book of Church Order and Discipline of the United Church of Jesus Christ (Apostolic)*. Washington, DC: 1965.

Schaller, Lyle E. *The Small Church is Different!* Nashville: Abingdon Press, 1982.

Simeon, Charles. *Evangelical Preaching*. Portland, OR: Multnomah Press, 1986.

Smith, Rockwell C. *Rural Ministry and the Changing Community*. Nashville: Abingdon Press, 1991.

Tozer, A. W. *Man: The Dwelling Place of God*. Harrisburg, PA: Christian Publications, 1966.

Willimon, William H. and Robert L. Wilson. *Preaching and Worship in the Small Church*. Nashville: Abingdon Press, 1982.

Wilson, John F. *Religion: A Preface*. Englewood Cliffs, NJ: Prentice-Hall, 1982.

Zikmund, Barbara Brown. *Discovering the Church*. Philadelphia: The Westminster Press, 1983.

WILLIAM H. JONES is a native of Freeman, Virginia, and received his early education in the Brunswick County Public Schools. He earned his Associate of Arts and Bachelor of Science degrees at The American University, Washington, DC; the Master of Education degree at Bowie State College (now University), Bowie, MD; the Master of Divinity and the Doctor of Ministry degrees from Howard University School of Divinity, Washington, DC.

Dr. Jones is a retired Metropolitan Police Officer from Washington, DC. He taught at St. Paul's College for many years where he held the position of Associate Professor of Religion and Education.

The author is the Administrative Bishop of The General Assembly of the St. James Churches of the Apostolic Faith and the Pastor of Great Branch United Church of Jesus Christ Apostolic in Rawlings, Virginia.

Dr. Jones and his wife, Queen Ester, are the parents of Rochann, Trudy, and Randy, and make their home in Rawlings, Virginia. Dr. Jones' hobbies include golfing, reading good books and playing the guitar.